PHOTOGRADE

A PHOTOGRAPHIC GRADING
GUIDE FOR UNITED STATES COINS

BY JAMES F. RUDDY

Member International Association of Professional Numismatists
Life Member American Numismatic Association
Member American Numismatic Society

All photographs by the author

Published by BOWERS AND RUDDY GALLERIES, INC.
6922 Hollywood Boulevard; Hollywood, California 90028

ACKNOWLEDGMENTS:

My grateful appreciation is extended to Jerry Cohen and Abner Kreisberg for their permission to photograph certain coins from their stock; to Q. David Bowers, my business associate in Bowers and Ruddy Galleries, Inc.; to John Murbach; and to my wife-secretary, Nancy, for their help in preparing this book.

Printing History:

First printing: August 1970
Second printing: September 1970
Third printing: October 1970
Fourth printing: January 1971
Fifth printing (with revisions): August 1972
Sixth printing: January 1973
Seventh printing: March 1974
Eighth printing: October 1974
Ninth printing: July 1975
Tenth printing: October 1976

"PHOTOGRADE"
has been designated as an
OFFICIAL GRADING GUIDE
by the
AMERICAN NUMISMATIC ASSOCIATION

TO NANCY

Her help and inspiration
cannot be graded highly enough

FOREWORD

In 1970, when I wrote the foreword to the first edition of *Photograde*, I noted that "I am confident that this volume will be enthusiastically received." It turned out that this was an understatement!

The book has been successful beyond Jim Ruddy's fondest expectation. Not only has there been the satisfaction of many printings (the book has become a numismatic best seller), there has been the satisfaction of acceptance by the numismatic field. Such critical acclaim as "A must for the library of every collector, beginner or advanced, of U.S. coins" (THE NUMISMATIST), "The most important innovation to hit the coin hobby in years " (NUMISMATIC NEWS), "Congratulations on 'Photograde.' Excellent work. Destined to become THE grading guide" (COIN WORLD) gives an idea of the welcome extended to *Photograde* by the hobby.

Here is the foreword I wrote for the first edition:

Grading is one of the most important and, at the same time, one of the most controversial, areas of numismatics. The difference between, say, Very Fine and Extremely Fine can make a large difference in value. Thus, in the rare coin marketplace grading information plays a leading role.

In the field of numismatic research grading is likewise useful. Common grading terminology permits the interchange of information in a concise manner. Writing about a rare variety of half cent, a scholar may note, "The finest specimen known to me grades Very Good." Another student, perhaps thousands of miles away, will then know he has a truly significant and perhaps very valuable piece should he encounter an Extremely Fine or other superior grade coin.

In the present volume James F. Ruddy draws upon his long experience as a coin dealer and as a collector to provide a wealth of information not hitherto available in print. Importantly, the author bases his grading system on the individual coins themselves. For the first time in any grading book such disparate coins as half dimes and silver dollars are graded by different standards, not by the same criteria.

It should be immediately obvious that if wear on the letters in the word LIBERTY is used as a grading focal point, then a coin with LIBERTY in relief (raised letters) — the U.S. twenty cent piece is an example — should be graded differently from a coin with LIBERTY incused (in sunken letters) — a Liberty seated half dime, for instance. Many early United States coins, particularly those struck during the first decade of the Mint's operations beginning in 1793, were made from hand-cut dies and were struck by methods far different from those in effect after steam presses were installed in 1836. Accordingly, these differences in striking methods must be recognized. A grading system applicable to a one cent piece of 1795 simply cannot be extended to include a cent of 1855 as well! As the reader will perceive as soon as he uses this book, Jim Ruddy knows and understands minting and minting procedures and imparts his knowledge to what he writes. In addition, he has painstakingly illustrated both the obverse and reverse of each coin — over 1,000 photographs in all. This feature, which up to now has not been available, is vitally important to the proper grading of a coin. The reader is the benefactor.

I am confident that this volume will be enthusiastically received by those on either side, buying or selling, of a numismatic transaction.

————Q. David Bowers

INTRODUCTION

People have been collecting coins for over 2000 years — making numismatics one of the oldest hobbies in the world. Before the 20th century most collectors graded their coins as being either "new" or "used." Rarely did the price of a coin dictate that a finer distinction in grading be made. Most often, coins could be purchased for a small premium over their face value.

The story today is much different. Since the numismatic boom began in the 1950's there has been an ever-increasing demand for rare coins. The supply remains constant as the mintage of a given issue cannot be changed. The natural result is a rise in values. This happened in the 1950's. And when it did, it became increasingly more important to grade coins carefully. The difference between Good and Fine might have meant $1 to $2 in the price of a particular coin in 1950. By the 1960's this same grading difference might have meant $25 to $50. In the future it may mean $50 to $100, or even more.

The numismatic industry of the 1950's fully realized the need to provide pricing and grading guides that would keep the collector well informed. Many new pricing catalogues were offered on the market, and the "Guide Book," long the standard pricing reference, was expanded and improved. A new weekly newspaper, *Coin World*, appeared in 1960 and offered a regular "Trends" section which featured coin values. *Numismatic News*, another weekly paper, offers its "Tele-Quotes" guide to values.

However, in the field of coin grading much less progress has been made. In 1958 Messrs. Brown and Dunn pioneered the standardization of grading by issuing a book which used line drawings to illustrate degrees of wear on a coin. A number of attempts were made by others to create standard grading reference books by using photographs of actual coins. Unfortunately, the photographic reproduction and, in a few cases, the grading information was inadequate to warrant the acceptance of any of these works as a standard.

Therefore today we are faced with the paradox of excellent progress in pricing information, but we have little that is new in grading guidelines since 1958. Pricing and grading are equally important as the value of a coin depends not only on its date and mintmark but on its grade as well. For example, if a coin catalogues $100 Fine, $200 Very Fine, and $300 Extremely Fine, not knowing whether a coin is Very Fine can be expensive. If you are offered a purported Very Fine for $200, and it is really only Fine, you've lost $100. On the other hand, if it is really Extremely Fine, you've made a windfall profit of $100! Check the prices in Fine, Very Fine, and Extremely Fine of a cent of 1793 or 1877, a 1916-D dime, or any one of hundreds of other examples, and you will see well the need for all collectors and dealers to have an accurate modern pictorial grading guide!

In 1968, after carefully considering the problems involved, I decided to write a book that would fill this need. I knew that four important factors were necessary to produce a successful photographic grading guide:

First was the access to hundreds of thousands of dollars' worth of coins needed for photography. For two years I systematically took pictures of every coin that came through my hands which best represented the average grade for its type. Additional coins and other help were provided by Jan Bronson, Jerry Cohen, Joe Flynn, Jr., and Abner Kreisberg. Q. David Bowers, my long-time business associate, provided other valuable assistance.

Next came research. Fortunately I have had nearly two decades of professional coin dealing experience to draw from. In this time I have graded tens of millions of dollars' worth of coins. My schooling and professional training was originally in scientific research. This background taught me to be precise and methodical on very minute details — important factors when formalizing a universal grading system.

Next came photography — by far the most formidable feature to master. The main problem was the extremes involved; the wide range in detail from About Good to About Uncirculated; the size differential from silver three cent pieces to silver dollars; the variations from a dark porous copper surface to a brilliant silver or gold one. Again, I was fortunate to have a background which was of immeasurable help. Before coins became my career I worked with the Physics Research Laboratory of Ansco Film Company. There I performed research on all aspects of photographic resolution. Even with this experience it took weeks of research to match the right camera, film, and light meter to produce the desired results. The camera I chose was an Exackta with a 50 mm. f 1.9 lens and a through-the-lens metering system. The film was picked, not to give "pretty" or "artistic-appearing" pictures, but to give extremely high resolution, high contrast, and fine grain features. Lighting was of paramount importance. Hundreds of test exposures utilizing dozens of various lighting conditions were tried before the first coin picture was taken. Experiments in film processing, background color, and the size of the printed coin picture were also necessary. I took over 5,000 photographs to achieve the desired results. In many instances a single exposure produced the perfect representation of a certain grade of that type. In other cases it took as many as 20 pictures to produce a single satisfactory one. There are over 1,000 different pictures in this book — many more than in any other grading guide.

Last, but not least, was printing. We have spared no expense to give you the highest quality printing which reproduces faithfully the original coin photographs. All pictures are printed in fine line screen which produces much finer detail than practically any other coin book of any type in the United States. We have used the highest quality coated paper. We could have cut corners here and there, but we didn't. We believe the book is much finer as a result.

———James F. Ruddy

HOW TO USE "PHOTOGRADE"

Every major type of United States coin is represented in this book. Different condition ranges are pictured and described. It's easy to check any coin with the uniform arrangement of pictures and descriptions. Simply follow the pictures with your coin until you come to the closest match. Then check the description beside that picture. Do the same for both the obverse and reverse. The terminology used to describe each condition is in the most basic, most concise form for quick reference. General descriptions are as follows:

ABOUT GOOD (usually abbreviated as Abt. G or AG) represents a very well worn coin which can still be identified, but barely, as to date and mint. (Note: Coins in Fair condition generally are identifiable only as to type)

GOOD (G) usually indicates an over-all clean-appearing coin with all lettering visible and with basic features outlined, except for coins in the 1790's and early 1800's.

VERY GOOD (VG) is probably one of the easiest grades to describe. In the majority of cases the word "LIBERTY" on the headband or shield can be used to determine the grade. When it is stated that a total of any three letters of "LIBERTY" verify this grade, it is taking into consideration the many diverse designs used on all our coins. In some cases three full letters may be visible, in other instances two full and two partial letters or even one full and four partial letters will show. Of course, it is important that all other features of both the obverse and reverse verify this grade.

FINE (F) condition is probably the most widely collected circulated grade. All of the major design is usually visible. The word "LIBERTY" (except on 20c pieces and Liberty seated silver dollars) is complete.

VERY FINE (VF). Some of the more intricate designs will be noticeable. A careful eye is needed to distinguish the differences between this grade and the next.

EXTREMELY FINE (EF or sometimes XF). Practically all details will be clearly visible.

ABOUT UNCIRCULATED (AU; or sometimes Almost Uncirculated). A coin that has seen a slight amount of circulation. Often some mint lustre will show in the field.

UNCIRCULATED. (Unc. or, if brilliant, BU). As an Uncirculated coin should have no wear it would be difficult to show the absence of wear in a photograph. In order to use *Photograde* to check a coin you believe to be Uncirculated, compare it to the About Uncirculated photograph and description. It should not show any of the traces of wear that are described. There are variations of the Uncirculated grade. Besides Brilliant Uncirculated (BU) and Toned Uncirculated, which are self-explanatory, there is Choice Uncirculated and Gem Uncirculated. Choice describes an above average Uncirculated specimen, well struck and with a minimum of minor bagmarks or minting defects. Gem is the finest obtainable, sharply struck and free of the usual minor bagmarks or minting defects. Another variation is Borderline Uncirculated. This is not an About Uncirculated coin which has seen circulation. Rather, it is a strictly Uncirculated coin with full mint lustre which may show envelope or cabinet friction, or possibly rubbing from an album slide or from contact with other coins in a mint bag.

PROOF. A coin in Proof condition should have no wear, friction, or rubbing of any kind unless it is impaired and so noted. Occasionally the mirrorlike surfaces will show minor hairlines, usually caused by rubbing with a cloth during a cleaning operation. These hairlines usually can only be seen with a magnifying glass but should be described as they reduce the value of a Proof coin 10% to 20%. A Matte Proof copper or nickel coin must have a square edge and rim plus a matte finish, not merely a matte-like appearance. The edge must look like this drawing around the entire circumference of the coin.

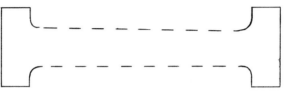

COLOR OF A COIN: An early copper coin showing original mint color is rare and should command a substantial premium. Recently, some unscrupulous people have devised a method of cleaning and toning copper coins to give them an artificial but deceptive-appearing "brilliant" surface. There is no way to accurately describe the varied results of this process. Your best protection is to deal only with a reputable dealer. A note of caution: "There is no Santa Claus in numismatics," Lee Hewitt, founder of *The Numismatic Scrapbook Magazine*, has said. Uncirculated and Proof coins traditionally sell for close to catalogue values or even over catalogue. Be wary of "bargains" described as Brilliant Uncirculated or BU. A polished AU coin which has been "processed" or polished to be sold as Brilliant Uncirculated will cost you, not save you, money! Such coins cost collectors hundreds of thousands of dollars each year!

Generally speaking, imperfections such as scratches, dents, edge bumps, and light corrosion will lower the condition of a coin by a full grade. Severe imperfections (holes, deep cuts, etc.) should be individually described and will further reduce a coin's grade.

SPLIT GRADES: Split grades are often advertised in order to more accurately describe a coin. A coin described as Good to Very Good (G-VG) may show evidence of a letter or two of "LIBERTY" (if that is the diagnostic grading feature) but not the total of three letters necessary to call it Very Good. A coin may have a Fine obverse but only a Very Good reverse (when obverse and reverse grades differ, it is customary to note this by a slash mark [/] as in F/VG) and should be described as such. This is not illogical. Sometimes a coin will be struck with a high protective rim on the obverse and a low rim on the reverse; a situation which causes the reverse to wear more quickly. Other examples exist. The more valuable a coin is, the more reason there is to use split grades. If a coin catalogues for $20 Good and $35 Very Good, then using the split grade of G-VG may make a difference of several dollars in value. This is an important consideration for both the buyer and seller.

INTERESTING VARIATIONS

We illustrate some interesting peculiarities and abnormalities that often appear on coins. Only a representative sampling can be shown as there are literally thousands of variations in the United States field.

DIE BREAKS: A die break is a raised protrusion on a coin caused when a die that has been broken (usually due to use) is used to strike that coin. Under minting pressure the coin metal is forced into the break in the die. A great number of astute collectors who collect by die varieties eagerly look for such die breaks for quick identification of the variety.

OVERDATES: Overdates are among the most sought-after coins in the United States series. If a die was unused or still in excellent condition at the end of a certain minting year the mint would occasionally repunch the date with the following year's digit(s) — thereby creating an overdate. There are dozens of different overdates in the United States series, of which about 20 sell for over $1000 each and five for over $5000 each. A few of the rare and unusual ones are shown here.

1798/7	1806/4	1888/7	1824/1	1823/2
$10	$2.50	1¢	$2.50	25¢

RE-ENGRAVED DATES: Not to be confused with overdates, re-engraved dates are caused when the die is repunched with the same date. This is ordinarily done to better reposition or to strengthen the date or individual numerals.

1795 50¢   1877-CC 25¢

ADJUSTMENT MARKS: In the very early days the crude minting facilities often produced planchets (metal coin blanks) that weighed too much. Those were frugal times and it was worthwhile to weigh every silver and gold planchet. If a planchet was overweight it would be scraped with a file to remove the extra metal. These file marks are often visible today on silver and gold coins of the 1790's and early 1800's. As they are of mint origin they should not detract from the monetary value of a coin.

INCUSATION OR CLASH MARKS: This interesting effect can be found on coins of all metals from 1793 to date. They are caused when the obverse and reverse dies come together without a coin planchet between them. The result is that some of the obverse design is permanently impressed in the reverse die and vice versa. Thereafter, every coin minted from these dies exhibits clash marks. Such clash marks do not affect a coin's value.

COUNTERFEIT COINS: Counterfeits exist in many fields: art, rare stamps, manuscripts, antiquities, and even stock certificates. Coins are no exception. Fortunately, stringent laws against counterfeiting United States coins keep the abuse to a minimum.

A few simple precautions will prevent the collector from being fooled by fake coins. Examine any suspicious coin carefully with a magnifying glass. If there are any tiny raised bubbles or raised rough areas this may indicate a cast or electrotype fake. If a suspicious coin has a non-reeded (plain) edge, inspect it for a fine line or seam running all the way around the coin. If such a seam exists, chances are good that the coin is an electrotype.

The simplest and most common method of testing a coin is to "ring" it. Balance the test coin on the tip of your index finger, hold it about six inches from your ear, and tap the edge very lightly with another coin (pocket change will do). If the coin does not have a bell-like ring there is a good possibility that it is a cast or an electrotype. Always do the "ring" test over a rug or soft area in case the coin drops.

Altered dates and mintmarks can often be detected by a magnifying glass. Struck counterfeits of gold coins are often very deceptive. The best way to avoid these is to deal with a reputable dealer. If a dealer won't guarantee the authenticity of his coins or sells a coin "as is" (without giving you the opportunity to have it checked by another expert), do business elsewhere. A fake coin is no bargain at any price and is, in fact, illegal to possess.

CLEANING: Before cleaning any coin, consider the subject carefully. Probably for every one coin "improved" by cleaning, ten have had their values lessened. Cleaning, when necessary, should be done only with nickel, silver, and gold coins in top grades. To clean any of the above-mentioned coins in grades less than About Uncirculated will produce an unnatural appearance that is generally not acceptable to most collectors. The cleaning of copper coins in any condition should be avoided unless it is necessary to remove an unsightly fingerprint or large carbon spots.

Use only a clear liquid "dip," not a paste, powder, or polish. Pour some dip, full strength, into a pliable plastic dish. Completely immerse the coin in the liquid. Do not leave the coin in the liquid longer than a few seconds. Immediately rinse the coin thoroughly under running cold water. Pat (do not rub) the coin dry with a soft absorbent cloth; a terrycloth towel is ideal. Holding the coin in your fingers and using a cotton swab may result in uneven cleaning. For copper coins use a mixture of half "dip" and half cold water. Always make sure your coins are thoroughly dry and at room temperature before storing them. Practice cleaning methods with low value coins!

It is sometimes desirable on circulated coins to remove the light film of oxidation that sometimes forms on copper. A gentle rubbing with a soft cloth lightly treated with a liquid product called "Care" will usually accomplish this task. Tape and most glues will come off with an application of acetone, a chemical available at drugstores.

IMPORTANT: The pictures in this book were chosen to represent the average of a particular grade or type. Naturally, variations in variety or striking must be taken into consideration, especially for coins minted before 1836 and for certain Denver and San Francisco issues in the 'teens and 1920's, for example. The reader must average the plus and minus factors when comparing a coin to the average picture. If any early large cent, for example, shows weak letters on the left side and very strong letters on the right, it must be assumed that the coin could not have been worn only on one portion of its surface. Examples such as this result from an improper strike, an uneven planchet, or improper die alignment. When grading a coin, take into consideration all of the features of each side — not just an isolated weak spot which was not a result of wear.

The American Numismatic Association

The American Numismatic Association (A.N.A.), an educational, non-profit organization, was founded in 1891. It is the most important numismatic association for a coin collector to join. Among the many benefits of belonging to the A.N.A. is the highly informative monthly publication, "The Numismatist."

For further information about joining the A.N.A., write to: American Numismatic Association; Box 2366; Colorado Springs, Colorado 80901.

EISENHOWER DOLLARS
1971 to date

VERY FINE

Obverse: There will be considerable wear on the cheek and jaw bones. Wear will also show on the neck and top of the head.

Reverse: There will be wear on the eagle's breast, left leg, and top feathers of the wings.

EXTREMELY FINE

Obverse: Slight wear will show on the cheek and jaw bones, and the top of the head.

Reverse: There will be slight wear on the eagle's breast, left leg, and tops of the wings.

ABOUT UNCIRCULATED

Obverse: Only a trace of wear will show on the cheek and jaw bones, and the top of the head.

Reverse: Only a trace of wear will appear on the eagle's breast, left leg, and top of the left wing.

COLONIAL COINS

I have separated the various styles and qualities of strikes among colonial coins into three basic groups.

The Connecticut copper coins pictured on this page represent the first group. These crudely-struck pieces were made from hand-crafted dies. Interesting, sometimes comical, diecutting errors abound in the Connecticut series, as do off-center strikes, incomplete or very weak design portions (due to striking, not to wear), and misaligned dies. Planchet imperfections are also quite common among Connecticut cents. Generally, the issues of 1785, the first year of Connecticut coinage, are the best from the standpoint of sharp striking. 1786 and 1787 issues are in lower relief and are less carefully struck. 1788 issues, the last year, are nearly always poorly and shallowly struck. Sometimes Connecticut cents, particularly issues of 1788, are found overstruck on other colonial and related issues — Nova Constellatio coppers and Irish halfpennies, for instance. All of these aspects contribute to the romance of Connecticut issues. Specialists find Connecticut cents to be fascinating and eagerly search for the over-300 die varieties known to exist.

Other popular colonials in this first group include all Massachusetts silver issues, Mark Newby pieces, Nova Eborac coppers, the Auctori Plebis token, Voce Populi coppers, and copper coins of Vermont. Like Connecticut coins, these issues were all made from hand-crafted, often crude (by later standards), dies.

GOOD	VG	FINE	VF

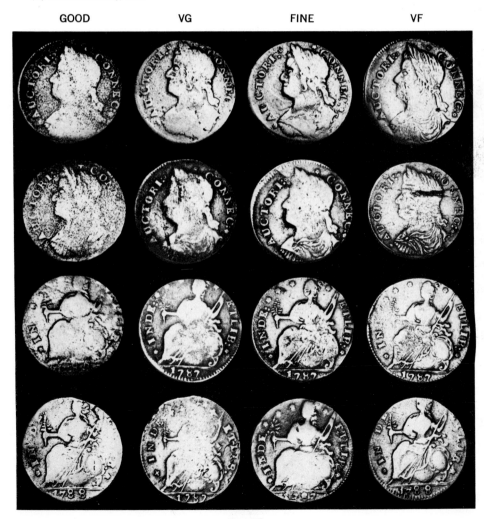

COLONIAL COINS

The second group of representative colonial coins contains coins that were originally struck with more care and precision than the first group. Included in the second group are New Jersey coppers (as illustrated here), Maryland silver issues, Rosa Americana coinage, Wood's or Hibernia pieces of 1722-1724, New York issues (except Nova Eborac and certain Machin's issues), Massachusetts cents and half cents of 1787 and 1788, Continental dollars, Nova Constellatio coppers, French Colonies issues, Chalmers' silver coinage, Elephant tokens, Virginia halfpennies, North American tokens, Pitt tokens, Washington pieces of United States origin, and Fugio cents.

Of these series, the Massachusetts copper coins were struck with the most uniformity. Well-centered and well-struck pieces are the rule, not the exception. Likewise, Hibernia and Virginia issues, both of which were made in England, are usually found well-struck. Elephant tokens vary: some are well-struck; others show weakness in portions. Nova Constellatio coppers are usually well-struck and well-centered, as are Continental dollars. Rosa Americana pieces, while well-made, are apt to have a porous surface due to the nature of the alloy, called "bath metal," used for most of these pieces. Fugio cent dies were well-made and are quite uniform in general appearance. Striking varied from one time to another, and some show weakness, especially on the center of the obverse.

New Jersey coppers, the type illustrated on this page, were generally well-struck. There were exceptions, and of the over-100 known die varieties, many, especially some of the rarer ones, are found with indistinct design portions.

GOOD	VG	FINE	VF

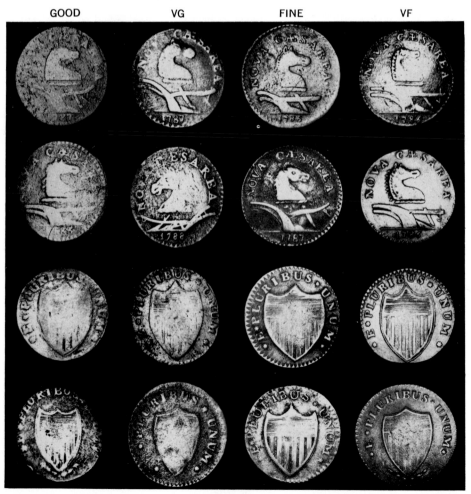

COLONIAL COINS

The third group of coins comprises well-struck issues, mostly of English origin. In England the state of the minting art, or at least the state of minting practice, was well advanced over that used in the United States during the c.1780-1820 period during which most coins in this third group were struck.

Illustrated on this page are Washington pieces of English origin, which serve to illustrate this group. Also in this group are the Bar Cents, Kentucky tokens, Myddelton tokens, Franklin Press tokens, and the Rhode Island Ship tokens. Most third-group coins are in Very Good or better grades when found today. Unlike most group-one and group-two colonials, many of the group-three coins are known in Uncirculated grade.

There are idiosyncrasies, to be sure, among coins of the third group. UNITY STATES "cents" are invariably found on striated planchets and with weak obverse lettering. 1793 Ship halfpennies usually display a die bulge at the lower right portion of the reverse. There are other examples. Still other issues (the Myddelton tokens and 1791 large-eagle and small-eagle cents are examples) nearly always are found perfectly struck and with excellent design detail.

Note: In recent years a number of forgeries of the 1776 Continental dollar, bar cent, and many other colonial issues have been issued, ostensibly for "souvenir" purposes. Occasionally these pieces, usually crude in appearance, find their way into numismatic channels. Most have a porous and pebbly surface and fail the "ring test" (see Counterfeit Coin section earlier). As is true when buying any rare or expensive coin, your best protection is to buy from an established professional dealer who guarantees what he sells. Why take chances?

VG	FINE	VF	EF

ABOUT GOOD

Obverse: Head and wreath will be distinct; a partial date must show. "LIBERTY" may not be distinct.

Reverse: The wreath will be almost complete but only a few letters of the legend will be readable.

GOOD

Obverse: Most of the lettering and design will be readable. The outline of the head will stand out boldly.

Reverse: The wreath will be complete. Half of the legend will be readable.

VERY GOOD

Obverse: Some hair detail will be visible. Date will be bold.

Reverse: The legend will be complete but some letters will be weak.

Note: The words "HALF CENT" were weakly struck on certain varieties and should not be used to determine condition.

FINE

Obverse: About 1/3 of the hair detail will show. All of the lettering will be clear.

Reverse: The leaves and berries in the wreath, although complete, will be quite flat.

VERY FINE

Obverse: At least half of the hair detail will be sharp. The hair ribbon will be distinct.

Reverse: The leaves in the wreath will be stronger but will not show leaf detail.

EXTREMELY FINE

Obverse: All major hair detail will show but will be worn on the high spots at the shoulder and to the right of the ear.

Reverse: The leaves in the wreath will show some detail and appear more rounded.

ABOUT UNCIRCULATED

Obverse: Only a trace of wear will show on Liberty's cheek and to the right of her ear.

Reverse: Most leaves will show full detail although some may not be fully struck up.

LIBERTY CAP HALF CENTS
1794-1797

ABOUT GOOD

Obverse: The head will be outlined but worn smooth. Lettering will be worn; date will partially show.

Reverse: A partial wreath and legend will show but will be very weak.

GOOD

Obverse: Most of "LIBERTY" will show. The date will be readable but may be quite weak.

Reverse: The wreath will be quite weak. At least half of the legend will be readable.

Note: The words "HALF CENT" were weakly struck on certain varieties and should not be used to determine condition.

VERY GOOD

Obverse: Some hair detail will show by the shoulder. "LIBERTY" will be strong but the date still may be weak (depending on the variety).

Reverse: The wreath will be complete. The legend will be complete (except on certain die varieties which were always weakly struck).

FINE

Obverse: About 1/3 of Liberty's hair will show plainly. The date will be clearly defined.

Reverse: The wreath will be bold but worn flat. There will not be any leaf detail.

VERY FINE

Obverse: At least half of Liberty's hair will be distinct.

Reverse: About half of the leaves will be individually separated but still show no detail.

Note: Weakness on only one area of a coin is probably due to the design or striking of that particular variety. This should be disregarded when determining condition. (This is applicable to any early U.S. coin.)

EXTREMELY FINE

Obverse: Almost full hair detail on Liberty's head, but definite wear will show around the ear and neck.

Reverse: All of the leaves will be separated from each other. There will be some leaf detail on the bottom leaves.

ABOUT UNCIRCULATED

Obverse: Wear will show only on the highest waves of hair around the ear and neck.

Reverse: Most of the leaves will show full detail and will be worn on the highest points only.

DRAPED BUST HALF CENTS
1800-1808

ABOUT GOOD

Obverse: An outline of the head and a partial date will show.

Reverse: A partial wreath and legend will show.

GOOD

Obverse: The head will be sharply outlined. All lettering will be readable although weak.

Reverse: The wreath will be complete. There may be wear on the tops of some of the letters of the legend.

VERY GOOD

Obverse: Hair detail will begin to show at the shoulder. "LIBERTY" will be strong.

Reverse: The lettering will be complete. Wreath will be bold but worn flat.

FINE

Obverse: Drapery on the bust will show but be worn at the top. About 1/2 of the hair detail will be visible. *Note: The bulge over the letters "RTY" is caused by a die break. Die breaks do not alter the condition of a coin.*

Reverse: A few leaves will be separated and show some detail.

VERY FINE

Obverse: About 2/3 of the hair detail will be visible. The top line of drapery will be complete to the hair.

Reverse: Almost all of the leaves will be separated. The bottom leaves will show some detail.

EXTREMELY FINE

Obverse: All hair detail will show but will be weak above the forehead and ear. Drapery will be well defined.

Reverse: Most of the leaves will show detail.

ABOUT UNCIRCULATED

Obverse: There will be slight wear on hair above the forehead and to the left of the ear.

Reverse: There will be only a trace of wear on the highest points of the leaves.

TURBAN HEAD HALF CENTS
1809-1836

ABOUT GOOD

Obverse: The rim will be worn down to the stars and date. Some "LIBERTY" letters may show.

Reverse: Only a partial legend will show. "HALF CENT" will be readable.

GOOD

Obverse: The head will be well outlined and may show a full "LIBERTY." Date will be bold.

Reverse: The rim will be worn down to the tops of the letters but all lettering will be readable.

VERY GOOD

Obverse: Hair detail and the ear will begin to show. There must be a full "LIBERTY."

Reverse: All letters will be complete. The wreath will be bold but worn almost flat.

FINE

Obverse: 2/3 of the hair detail will show. Hair curl on neck will show clearly although hair above the forehead will be worn. "LIBERTY" will be strong.

Reverse: Most of the leaves will be separated; a few will show detail.

VERY FINE

Obverse: All hair will show but will be weak around Liberty's face and below ear.

Reverse: About half of the leaves will show detail and all will be separated.

EXTREMELY FINE

Obverse: Full hair will show but there will be wear on the higher points.

Reverse: All of the leaves will show some detail.

ABOUT UNCIRCULATED

Obverse: The hair detail will be very sharp with only a trace of wear on the higher points.

Reverse: Slight wear will show on only the highest points of the top leaves.

HALF CENT TOKEN 1837

FINE

Obverse: There will be a trace of detail on the eagle's wings.

Reverse: The leaves in the wreath will be separated and a few will show detail.

Note: This token is rarely found in conditions below Fine.

VERY FINE

Obverse: About 2/3 of the eagle's wings will show feathers.

Reverse: About half of the leaves will show detail.

EXTREMELY FINE

Obverse: All of the eagle's feathers will show but will be worn on the high points.

Reverse: More detail will show on the leaves.

ABOUT UNCIRCULATED

Obverse: There will be a trace of wear only on the highest points of the feathers. The top of the eagle's right wing may be flatly struck.

Reverse: Slight wear will be visible on only the highest points of the leaves.

BRAIDED HAIR HALF CENTS
1840-1857

VERY GOOD

Obverse: Full "LIBERTY" but "L" will be weak. About half of the hair detail will be visible but not sharp.

Reverse: The wreath will be outlined with the leaves worn flat.

FINE

Obverse: Hair cord will be sharp. Hair around the face will be outlined but worn.

Reverse: Most leaves will be separated and begin to show some detail.

VERY FINE

Obverse: All hair detail will show but will be weak about the ear and by the neck.

Reverse: About half of the leaves will show detail.

EXTREMELY FINE

Obverse: All hair detail will be well outlined with wear only on the higher points.

Reverse: All of the leaves will be detailed but will show definite wear.

ABOUT UNCIRCULATED

Obverse: Only the slightest trace of wear will show on Liberty's hair above her ear.

Reverse: Slight wear will be visible on only the highest points of the leaves.

1793 CHAIN LARGE CENT

FAIR

Obverse: Identifiable as to type by the distinct head type. No date will show.
Reverse: The chain must show.

ABOUT GOOD

Obverse: The head will be well worn. A partial date must show.

Reverse: The chain will be well defined. Some of the legend will be readable.

GOOD

Obverse: The head will be outlined although worn flat. The date will show but may be worn at the bottom or weakly struck.

Reverse: Most of the legend will be readable, including the denomination "ONE CENT."

VERY GOOD

Obverse: The date will be full. Head will be well outlined.

Reverse: All of the lettering will be readable although some letters will be weak.

FINE

Obverse: The tips of Liberty's hair will be well outlined but the other 2/3 of her hair will be worn smooth.

Note: The head almost always comes weakly struck. This must be considered when grading Chain cents.

Reverse: The chain and center lettering will be bold. All other lettering will be distinct.

VERY FINE

Obverse: About half of Liberty's hair will show detail. Her ear may not show on the average weakly struck piece.

Reverse: The chain and center lettering will be very bold.

EXTREMELY FINE

Obverse: Hair below Liberty's ear and above her head will show definite wear.

Reverse: The links of the chain will be well rounded with wear showing only on the high points.

ABOUT UNCIRCULATED

Obverse: Wear will be visible only on the highest points of hair around Liberty's face.

Reverse: Only a trace of wear will be visible on the highest points of the chain.

1793 WREATH LARGE CENT

ABOUT GOOD

Obverse: A partial date must show.
Reverse: Most of the wreath will be clear with only a few letters visible.

GOOD

Obverse: Head will be worn completely flat. Date and "LIBERTY" will show but may be weak.
Reverse: The rim may be worn down into some of the letters.

VERY GOOD

Obverse: All letters and date will show clearly. 1/3 of the hair detail will be distinct.
Reverse: All of the lettering will be clear (but some may be weak due to striking).

FINE

Obverse: All lettering and date will be sharp. About half of the hair detail will be visible.
Reverse: The wreath will be well outlined but flat. Lettering will be sharp.

VERY FINE

Obverse: About 2/3 of the hair detail will show.
Reverse: The beaded border will be sharp. Leaves will be separated but worn flat.

EXTREMELY FINE

Obverse: There will be wear on the highest points of hair from the forehead to the shoulder.

Reverse: There will be a slight roundness to the leaves.

ABOUT UNCIRCULATED

Obverse: The hair detail will be complete but worn on the highest points to the left of the ear and neck.

Reverse: The leaves will be well rounded with wear only on the highest points.

LIBERTY CAP LARGE CENTS
1793-1796

ABOUT GOOD

Obverse: The head and some lettering will be visible. Date will be readable although weak.

Reverse: Most of the wreath will be clear with only a few letters visible.

GOOD

Obverse: The head will be well defined. Most of the lettering and date will be clearly readable.

Reverse: The rim may be worn down into some of the letters (which will be visible but weak).

Note: The words "ONE CENT" were weakly struck on certain varieties and should not be used to determine condition.

VERY GOOD

Obverse: Some hair detail will show. All lettering will be distinct. *Note: There may be weakness in spots due to the methods of striking these early coins.*

Reverse: All of the lettering will be clear.

FINE

Obverse: About half of Liberty's hair will show clearly.

Reverse: The wreath will be well outlined but flat.

VERY FINE

Obverse: The hair behind Liberty's ear and above her forehead will be worn but the rest of the hair will be detailed.

Reverse: The leaves will be separated but show very little detail.

EXTREMELY FINE

Obverse: All major hair detail will be visible with wear only on high spots.

Reverse: The leaves will be well defined with some leaves showing detail.

ABOUT UNCIRCULATED

Obverse: All of the hair detail will be strong but will show a trace of wear on the higher points.

Reverse: Leaf detail will be quite distinct with only slight wear visible.

DRAPED BUST LARGE CENTS
1796-1807

ABOUT GOOD

Obverse: The head will be outlined and the date will be readable but weak.

Reverse: Half of the lettering will be visible.

GOOD

Obverse: The head will be distinctly outlined.

Reverse: All of the letters will be readable although the rim may be worn down into some of them because of uneven striking.

VERY GOOD

Obverse: About 1/3 of the hair detail will show. The date will be bold.

Reverse: All letters will show. The wreath will be outlined but show no detail.

FINE

Obverse: About 2/3 of the hair detail will show. The hair will be smooth above Liberty's forehead, the top of her head, and to the left of her neck.

Reverse: Some of the leaves will show individual separation.

VERY FINE

Obverse: Almost all of the hair will be visible but will be worn flat on the higher points.

Note: Coins made over 150 years ago were often unevenly struck or have imperfections that cannot be standardized in any grading book.

Reverse: Each individual leaf will be well defined with little detail showing.

EXTREMELY FINE

Obverse: Full hair will show but have wear on the tips of the curls and to the right of her forehead.

Reverse: Most of the leaves will show detail but will be worn on all of the high spots.

ABOUT UNCIRCULATED

Obverse: All hair detail will be sharp. There will only be a trace of wear on the highest points of hair.

Reverse: All of the leaves will show detail or be well rounded. Wear will show only on the very highest points.

TURBAN HEAD LARGE CENTS
1808-1814

ABOUT GOOD

Obverse: The rim will be worn down into the stars. Date will be readable but weak.

Reverse: Half of the lettering will be visible.

GOOD

Obverse: The date and stars will be clear. The head will be distinctly outlined. A partial "LIBERTY" may show.

Reverse: All of the letters will be readable although the rims may be worn down into some of them because of uneven striking.

VERY GOOD

Obverse: About 1/3 of the hair detail will show, and the ear will be visible. A full "LIBERTY" will show.

Reverse: All of the letters will show although some may be weakly struck. The wreath will be flat but well defined.

FINE

Obverse: About 2/3 of the hair will show, but weakly. Hair around the face will be worn almost smooth. The ear will be sharp.

Reverse: The top leaves of the wreath will be worn flat.

VERY FINE

Obverse: All of the hair will show but be quite weak in detail.

Reverse: The top leaves and bow will show some detail.

EXTREMELY FINE

Obverse: Full hair will show but will be worn above the eye, above "LIBERTY," and on the tips of the curls.

Reverse: The high points of the leaves will show wear.

ABOUT UNCIRCULATED

Obverse: The hair will be quite sharp with only a trace of wear on the higher points. *Note: The hair above "LIBERTY" was usually weakly struck.*

Reverse: There will be only a trace of wear on the highest points of the leaves and wreath bow.

CORONET TYPE LARGE CENTS
1816-1839

ABOUT GOOD

Obverse: The rim will be worn down into the stars. The date will be readable but weak.

Reverse: Half of the lettering will be visible.

GOOD

Obverse: The date and the stars will be clear. The head will be distinctly outlined. A partial "LIBERTY" may show.

Reverse: All of the letters will be readable although the rim may be worn down into some of them because of uneven striking.

VERY GOOD

Obverse: About 1/3 of the hair detail will be visible. The hair cords will begin to show. "LIBERTY" will be full.

Reverse: All of the letters will show strongly. The wreath will be flat but well defined.

FINE

Obverse: Most of the major hair detail will be visible. The hair cords will show weakly.

Reverse: The top leaves and the wreath bow will be worn flat.

VERY FINE

Obverse: The hair will be worn flat on the higher points. Both hair cords will show plainly.

Reverse. The top leaves and bow will show some detail.

EXTREMELY FINE

Obverse: The hair will be sharp with weakness showing only above the forehead and at the highest point on top of the head. Hair cords will stand out sharply.

Reverse: The highest points of the leaves will show wear.

ABOUT UNCIRCULATED

Obverse: Only a trace of wear will be visible on the higher points of the hair.

Reverse: There will be a trace of wear only on the highest points of the leaves and wreath bow.

BRAIDED HAIR LARGE CENTS
1840-1857

ABOUT GOOD

Obverse: The date and stars will be weak but visible.

Reverse: Half of the lettering will be visible.

GOOD

Obverse: The date and stars will be clear. The head will be distinctly outlined. A partial "LIBERTY" may show.

Reverse: All of the lettering will be readable although the rim may be worn down to the tops of some of the letters.

VERY GOOD

Obverse: "LIBERTY" will be readable but "L" and "I" will be weak. About 1/3 of the hair detail will be clear.

Reverse: All of the lettering will show strongly. The wreath will be flat but well defined.

FINE

Obverse: About 2/3 of the hair detail will show. Hair above the eye will show but be worn. Beaded hair cords will be sharp.

Reverse: The top leaves will be worn flat.

VERY FINE

Obverse: All hairlines will be complete but some will be weak, especially on top of the head. Hair above the eye and the beaded hair cords will be well defined.

Reverse: The top leaves will show some detail.

EXTREMELY FINE

Obverse: The hair above the ear will be slightly worn.

Reverse: The highest points of the leaves will show wear.

ABOUT UNCIRCULATED

Obverse: Only a trace of wear will show on the highest points of the hair above the ear and eye.

Reverse: There will be a trace of wear only on the highest points of the leaves and wreath bow.

FLYING EAGLE CENTS
1856-1858

ABOUT GOOD

Obverse: The date will be weak but readable.

Reverse: The rim will be worn down into the wreath.

GOOD

Obverse: The lettering and the date will be readable although the rim may be worn down to the tops of the letters.

Reverse: The wreath will be completely outlined but worn flat.

VERY GOOD

Obverse: About 1/3 of the feathers on the eagle will show but will be weak.

Reverse: The wreath will show some detail but be worn smooth on top.

FINE

Obverse: About half of the feathers on the eagle will show. The detail of the eagle's head will be very clear.

Reverse: More detail will appear on the wreath.

VERY FINE

Obverse: About 3/4 of the feathers will show sharply. The eagle's tail feathers will be complete. There will be considerable flatness on the eagle's breast.

Reverse: The ends of the leaves will be worn smooth. *Note: The words "ONE CENT" are sometimes weak due to striking.*

EXTREMELY FINE

Obverse: There will be wear on the eagle's breast and left wing tip. All other details will be sharp.

Reverse: There will be wear on the high points of the leaves and ribbon bow.

ABOUT UNCIRCULATED

Obverse: There will be only a trace of wear on the eagle's breast and left wing tip. *Note: Weakness of lettering and date may appear on some 1857 cents due to striking.*

Reverse: Only a trace of wear will show on the highest points of the leaves and bow.

INDIAN HEAD CENTS
1859-1909

ABOUT GOOD

Obverse: The rim will be worn down well into the letters. The date will be weak but readable.

Reverse: The rim will be worn down into the wreath.

GOOD

Obverse: The outline of the Indian will be distinct. "LIBERTY" will not show on the headband. The rim may be worn down to the tops of the letters.

Reverse: The wreath will be completely outlined but worn flat.

VERY GOOD

Obverse: A total of any three letters of "LIBERTY" will show. This can be a combination of two full letters plus two half letters as not all dates of Indian cents wore uniformly.

Reverse: The wreath will begin to show some detail. *Note: The bottom of the "N" in "ONE" may be weak due to striking.*

FINE

Obverse: A full "LIBERTY" will be visible but it will not be sharp.

Reverse: The top part of the leaves will be worn smooth. The ribbon bow will show considerable wear.

VERY FINE

Obverse: A full sharp "LIBERTY" will be visible even though there is some wear. The feathers will be worn on the tips. *Note: Indian cents cannot be graded by the diamond designs on the obverse as this feature was not always sharply struck.*

Reverse: There will be more detail in the leaves and ribbon bow.

EXTREMELY FINE

Obverse: There must be a full sharp "LIBERTY." The ends of the feathers (except on certain weakly struck issues, such as 1859-1864 copper-nickel pieces) will be sharply detailed.

Reverse: There will be wear on the high points of the leaves and ribbon bow.

ABOUT UNCIRCULATED

Obverse: Only a trace of wear will show on the highest points such as above the ear and the lowest curl of hair.

Reverse: Only a trace of wear will show on the highest points of the leaves and ribbon bow.

LINCOLN HEAD CENTS
1909 to date

ABOUT GOOD

Obverse: The rim will be worn down into the letters. Date and mintmark will be weak but readable.

Reverse (1909-1958): The rim will be worn down into the letters and the wheat stalks.

GOOD

Obverse: Letters in the legend may be touching the rim. The date will be full.

Reverse (1909-1958): The wheat stalks will be worn smooth but distinctly outlined.

VERY GOOD

Obverse: All letters in the legend will be sharp and clear. A few hair details will begin to show.

Reverse (1909-1958): About half of the lines in the upper wheat stalks will show.

FINE

Obverse: Lincoln's ear and bow tie will be clearly visible.

Reverse (1909-1958): The parallel lines in the upper wheat stalks will show plainly and be separated even though worn. One side or the other may show a weak area at the top of the stalk.

VERY FINE

Obverse: The ear and bow tie will be sharp. All of Lincoln's hair will be visible but worn. The cheek and jaw details on Lincoln's face will show clearly.

Reverse (1909-1958): The lines in the wheat stalks will be full and will show no weak spots.

EXTREMELY FINE

Obverse: There will be wear only on the high points of Lincoln's head and face.

Reverse (1909-1958): The lines in the wheat stalks will be very bold and clearly defined.

Note: Many "D" and "S" coins of the 1920's are weakly struck, and should be graded by the best side. 1922 "Plain" is very weakly struck and lacks sharp detail, even in the higher grades.

ABOUT UNCIRCULATED

Obverse: Only the slightest trace of wear will show on the high points of Lincoln's cheek and jaw.

Reverse (1909-1958): Only a trace of wear will show on the wheat stalks.

TWO CENT PIECES 1864-1873

ABOUT GOOD

Obverse: The rim will be worn down into the date and wreath.

Reverse: Half of the lettering will be visible.

GOOD

Obverse: The date will be clear. A partial "IN GOD WE TRUST" must show.

Reverse: All of the lettering will be visible although a few letters may be weak.

VERY GOOD

Obverse: The motto words "IN GOD" and "TRUST" will show clearly. There will be a slight trace of the word "WE."

Reverse: All of the lettering will be bold. Half of the wheat grains will show.

FINE

Obverse: The motto "IN GOD WE TRUST" will show completely, but "WE" will be quite weak.

Reverse: Almost all of the wheat grains will show.

VERY FINE

Obverse: The entire motto, including "WE," will be easily readable.

Note: The horizontal lines in the shield may not be complete even on higher grades due to striking.

Reverse: All of the wheat grains will show plainly.

EXTREMELY FINE

Obverse: The full motto will be boldly readable. The leaves will show considerable detail especially at the bottom.

Reverse: The high points of the wreath and ribbon will show wear.

ABOUT UNCIRCULATED

Obverse: There will be only a trace of wear on the high points of the design — such as the tips of the leaves, the arrow points, and the word "WE."

Reverse: There will be a trace of wear only on the highest points of the wreath and ribbon.

NICKEL THREE CENT PIECES
1865-1889

ABOUT GOOD

Obverse: The rim will be worn down into some of the letters.

Reverse: The rim will be worn down into the wreath.

GOOD

Obverse: The rim will be worn down to the tops of the letters.

Reverse: The leaves in the wreath will be flat and only a few will be separated.

VERY GOOD

Obverse: There will be a full rim. Very little hair detail will show.

Reverse: There will be a full rim. About half of the leaves will be separated from each other.

FINE

Obverse: About 1/3 of the hair detail will show.

Note: This coin usually comes with weak hair detail over the ear even on higher grade coins.

Reverse: All of the leaves will be separated. Some of the lines will show weakly in the Roman numeral III.

VERY FINE

Obverse: 2/3 of the hair detail will show plainly.

Reverse: The lines will be sharper.

Note: This coin often comes with weakly struck lines even on higher grade pieces.

EXTREMELY FINE

Obverse: The upper hair and lower curls should be very sharp.

Reverse: All of the lines will be boldly visible in at least one figure of the Roman numeral III. There will be wear only on the tips of the leaves.

ABOUT UNCIRCULATED

Obverse: Only the slightest trace of wear will show on the hair curls and the hair above the forehead.

Reverse: Only a trace of wear will show on the wreath and Roman numeral III.

SHIELD NICKELS 1866-1883

ABOUT GOOD

Obverse: The rim will be worn down into the letters and wreath.

Reverse: The rim will be worn down into the letters.

GOOD

Obverse: The date and all letters should be clear although the rim may be worn down to the tops of the letters. Leaves will be flat.

Reverse: The rim will be worn down to the tops of the letters.

VERY GOOD

Obverse: The leaves will show slight detail. Some of the horizontal lines in the shield will show.

Reverse: There will be a full rim.

Note: The numeral "5" may be weak in spots due to striking. This should not affect the grade.

FINE

Obverse: Individual leaves will be separated but worn smooth halfway from the tips to the center of the leaves.

Reverse: The stars, with a few lines showing, will be very bold.

VERY FINE

Obverse: The leaves will be more defined and clearly separated.

Reverse: Most of the lines in the stars will be complete. *Note: If some stars are strong and some weak, determine grade by the strong ones. (Certain issues have all stars weakly struck — in which case determine grade by the obverse only.)*

EXTREMELY FINE

Obverse: The leaves will stand out in bold relief with most of the center lines showing clearly.

Note: The horizontal lines in the shield may be incomplete because of striking even on higher grades and should not affect the grading.

Reverse: The strongest stars will show full sharp lines.

ABOUT UNCIRCULATED

Obverse: Only a trace of wear will show on the tips of the leaves and on the highest points of the shield.

Reverse: The stars will show only a trace of wear (but may be weak, as noted, due to striking).

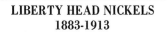

LIBERTY HEAD NICKELS
1883-1913

ABOUT GOOD

Obverse: The rim will be worn down into the stars and/or the date.

Reverse: The figure "V" and the wreath will be visible.

GOOD

Obverse: Liberty will be outlined but the legend "LIBERTY" will not show on her headband.

Reverse: The rim may be worn down to the tops of the letters. "E PLURIBUS UNUM" will be barely visible.

VERY GOOD

Obverse: A total of any three letters of "LIBERTY" must show. This could be a combination of two full letters plus two half letters as not all dates of Liberty nickels wore uniformly.

Reverse: The wreath will be sharply outlined. "E PLURIBUS UNUM" will show weakly.

FINE

Obverse: A full "LIBERTY" must be readable, including the letter "I." About half of the hair detail will be visible.

Reverse: Detail will begin to appear in the wreath. "E PLURIBUS UNUM" will be strong.

VERY FINE

Obverse: "LIBERTY" will be complete and bold. The hair will show about 75% detail.

Reverse: Partial detail will show on the leaves of the wreath and the ear of corn.

EXTREMELY FINE

Obverse: "LIBERTY" will be very bold. All of the details will be visible but may be weak on the high points above the ear and forehead.

Reverse: There will be wear on the high points of the wreath and ear of corn.

ABOUT UNCIRCULATED

Obverse: There will be only the slightest trace of wear on the highest portion of the hair above the ear and forehead.

Reverse: There will be only a trace of wear on the highest portions of the wreath.

BUFFALO NICKELS 1913-1938

ABOUT GOOD

Obverse: The rim will be worn down well into the letters. Only a partial date will show, but date must be recognizable.

Reverse: The rim will be worn down into the letters.

GOOD

Obverse: The rim will be worn down into the tops of the letters of "LIBERTY." The date will be readable but some of the numbers will be well worn.

Reverse: The rim may be worn down into the tops of the letters. The horn need not show.

VERY GOOD

Obverse: The rim may touch the tops of the letters of "LIBERTY." The date will be distinct.

Reverse: There will be a full rim. Half of the horn will show. The buffalo's back will be almost smooth.

FINE

Obverse: "LIBERTY" will be separated from the rim. The date will be very bold.

Reverse: 2/3 of the horn will show. The major detail on the buffalo's back will show.

VERY FINE

Obverse: The hair braid and cheek will show some detail but be flat on the high spots.

Reverse: There will be a full horn but the top may not be well outlined. The hair on the buffalo's head will be well worn.

EXTREMELY FINE

Obverse: The hair braid and face details on the Indian are now very bold with only slight wear on the high points.

Reverse: A full sharp horn will show. The tail will show on the hip. Flat spots of wear will show on the head, upper front leg, and on the hip.

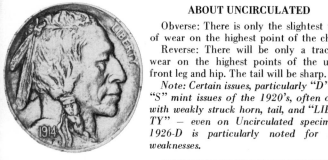

ABOUT UNCIRCULATED

Obverse: There is only the slightest trace of wear on the highest point of the cheek.

Reverse: There will be only a trace of wear on the highest points of the upper front leg and hip. The tail will be sharp.

Note: Certain issues, particularly "D" and "S" mint issues of the 1920's, often come with weakly struck horn, tail, and "LIBERTY" — even on Uncirculated specimens. 1926-D is particularly noted for such weaknesses.

JEFFERSON NICKELS
1938 to date

GOOD

Obverse: The rim will be worn down to the tops of the letters. The head will be worn flat.

Reverse: Monticello will be worn smooth.

VERY GOOD

Obverse: The rim will be worn down to the tops of the letters. Only the hair on the back of the head will show detail.

Reverse: The four main pillars of Monticello will show but be very weak.

FINE

Obverse: About half of the major hair detail will show. The cheek will be worn flat.

Reverse: The two outer pillars will be well outlined. The two inner pillars will show but may not be complete from top to bottom.

VERY FINE

Obverse: About 3/4 of the major hair detail will show.

Reverse: All four pillars will be well defined. The archway above the pillars will show major detail.

EXTREMELY FINE

Obverse: All of the hair detail will show but will be worn on the high points. The cheekbone will be well rounded but show wear.

Reverse: All details on Monticello will show except the triangle in the arch above the pillars.

ABOUT UNCIRCULATED

Obverse: There will be a trace of wear on the cheekbone and higher points of the hair.

Reverse: All details on Monticello will be sharp, including the triangle. There will be only a trace of wear on the highest points.

Note: The steps on Monticello will be full only on very well struck pieces and should command a premium price.

SILVER THREE CENT PIECES
1851-1873

ABOUT GOOD

Obverse: About half of the lettering will show.

Reverse: The rim will be worn down well into the stars.

GOOD

Obverse: The rim may be worn down into a few letters and part of the date.

Reverse: The rim will be worn down to the tops of the stars.

VERY GOOD

Obverse: The letters and date will be full. The shield in the center of the star may not be fully outlined.

Reverse. The stars will be well outlined and separated from the rim.

FINE

Obverse: The shield will be complete.

Reverse: The design in the "C" will begin to show.

VERY FINE

Obverse: The star will be bold but show definite signs of wear on the high points and tips.

Reverse: The design in the "C" will be separated inside the circles.

EXTREMELY FINE

Obverse: The star and shield will be very bold.

Reverse: The design in the "C" will now be well rounded.

ABOUT UNCIRCULATED

Obverse: The star will show only a trace of wear on the top of each star point. *Note: The center of the shield may be weak due to striking on some pieces.*

Reverse: Only a trace of wear will appear on the design in the "C" and on the Roman numeral III.

FLOWING HAIR HALF DIMES
1794-1795

ABOUT GOOD

Obverse: The rim will be worn down into the stars, legend, and/or date.

Reverse: The rim will be worn down well into the lettering and design.

GOOD

Obverse: The bust will be outlined but will not show detail. The date, stars, and lettering will be readable.

Reverse: The rim will be worn into the tops of a few letters. The eagle will be outlined but show no detail.

VERY GOOD

Obverse: Some detail will show on the ends of the hair. The major facial details will show.

Reverse: All of the letters will be fully visible. The wings will show a few feather details.

FINE

Obverse: About half of the major hair detail will show.

Reverse: A few more feathers will show in the wings. The leaves will be worn flat.

VERY FINE

Obverse: The hair above Liberty's forehead will be outlined and will show major details.

Reverse: About half of the feathers will show. The leaves will be well rounded but show no detail.

EXTREMELY FINE

Obverse: All of the hair detail will show. There will be wear only on the high waves of hair.

Reverse: Most of the feathers will show in the wings. *Note: Because of striking, the breast rarely comes with full feather detail even on Uncirculated specimens. Some specimens have weakly struck wing feathers as well.*

ABOUT UNCIRCULATED

Obverse: Only a trace of wear will be visible on the high waves of hair around the face and ear.

Note: There may be weakness due to striking on the hair behind the ear.

Reverse: Only a trace of wear will appear on the head and top edges of the eagle's wings.

DRAPED BUST HALF DIMES
1796-1805

(For 1800-1805 reverses see page 55)

ABOUT GOOD

Obverse: The rim will be worn down into the stars, "LIBERTY," and/or the date. The head will be worn flat.

Reverse: The rim will be worn down well into the letters and design.

GOOD

Obverse: The rim will be worn down to the tops of the stars. A few letters of "LIBERTY" may be worn. Head will be well outlined.

Reverse: The rim will be worn down to the tops of some of the letters. The eagle will be outlined but show no detail.

VERY GOOD

Obverse: About 1/4 of the hair detail will show, mostly in the lower curls. Some evidence of drapery lines will show.

Reverse: All of the letters will be fully visible.

FINE

Obverse: About half of the hair detail will show.

Reverse: Some feathers will show in the wings.

VERY FINE

Obverse: About 3/4 of the hair detail will show.

Note: Drapery lines across Liberty's bust cannot be used to determine grade as they vary greatly in sharpness from coin to coin because of striking.

Reverse: About half of the wing feathers will show.

EXTREMELY FINE

Obverse: All of the major detail of the hair will show. Wear will be visible to the left of the forehead.

Reverse: Most of the feathers will show in the wings. *Note: The breast feathers are rarely visible because of striking, even on high grade specimens.*

ABOUT UNCIRCULATED

Obverse: Only a slight trace of wear will be visible on Liberty's bust, shoulder, and hair left of her forehead. *Note: Hair may be flat to the left of Liberty's neck due to striking.*

Reverse: Only a trace of wear will appear on the head and top edges of the wings.

CAPPED HALF DIMES
1829-1837

ABOUT GOOD

Obverse: The rim will be worn down into the stars and/or date. The head will be worn smooth.

Reverse: About half of the lettering will be visible.

GOOD

Obverse: The head will be flat. At least half of "LIBERTY" will be readable.

Reverse: All of the lettering will be complete. The eagle will be flat. There may not be a full "E PLURIBUS UNUM."

VERY GOOD

Obverse: There will be a full "LIBER-TY." About half of the hair detail will be visible.

Reverse: "E PLURIBUS UNUM" will be complete. There will be a few feathers showing in the eagle's left wing.

FINE

Obverse: The lower drapery folds will be sharp. About 3/4 of the hair detail will show.

Reverse: About half of the feathers in the eagle's wings will show.

VERY FINE

Obverse: All of the major details of the hair will show, except the curl on the neck. The ear and drapery clasp will show clearly.

Reverse: 3/4 of the feathers will show. The neck and right leg will show considerable wear.

EXTREMELY FINE

Obverse: All of the hair will be sharp with wear only on the highest curls. The curl on the neck will show.

Reverse: All of the feathers will show but will be worn on the highest points. The edges of both wings will be worn.

ABOUT UNCIRCULATED

Obverse: There will be only a trace of wear on the highest points of the hair above the forehead and ear.

Reverse: There will be only a trace of wear on the eagle's claws, neck, and along the edges of the wings. *Note: The right wing of the eagle and the center of "E PLURIBUS UNUM" may be flat due to striking.*

HALF DIMES 1837-1838
(no stars)

ABOUT GOOD

Obverse: The rim will be worn down into the field and may be worn into the date and/or head.

Reverse: About half of the lettering will be visible.

GOOD

Obverse: There will be a full outline of Liberty. The shield will be worn smooth.

Reverse: The rim will be worn down to the tops of some of the letters.

VERY GOOD

Obverse: A total of any three letters of "LIBERTY" will be visible on the shield.

Reverse: There will be a full rim. The leaves in the wreath will be outlined but not well defined.

FINE

Obverse: There will be a full "LIBERTY" (including the letters "BE") on the shield, but it will not be sharp.

Reverse: The leaves will be separated but little detail will show.

VERY FINE

Obverse: "LIBERTY" will be sharp. Only the deepest folds of Liberty's gown will be visible.

Reverse: About half of the leaves will show detail.

EXTREMELY FINE

Obverse: There will be wear on Liberty's breast and legs.

Reverse: All of the leaves will show detail but will be worn on the ends.

ABOUT UNCIRCULATED

Obverse: Only a trace of wear will appear on Liberty's breast and knees.

Note: The horizontal lines of the shield often come weak, even on higher grades.

Reverse: Only a trace of wear will be visible on the ribbon bow and the tips of the leaves.

LIBERTY SEATED HALF DIMES
1838-1859

ABOUT GOOD

Obverse: The rim will be worn down into the date and/or stars.

Reverse: About half of the lettering will be visible.

GOOD

Obverse: There will be a full outline of Liberty. The shield will be worn smooth.

Reverse: The rim will be worn down to the tops of some of the letters.

Note: Half dimes of 1838-1859 are usually seen with the reverse weaker than the obverse by at least one grade. This is due to the shallower die relief of the reverse.

VERY GOOD

Obverse: A total of any three letters (can be two full letters plus two half letters) of "LIBERTY" will be visible on the shield.

Reverse: There will be a full rim. The leaves in the wreath will be outlined but not well defined.

FINE

Obverse: There will be a full "LIBERTY" on the shield, but it will not be sharp.

Reverse: The leaves will be separated but will have little detail.

VERY FINE

Obverse: "LIBERTY" will be sharp. Only the deepest folds of Liberty's gown will be visible.

Reverse: About half of the leaves will show detail.

EXTREMELY FINE

Obverse: There will be wear on Liberty's head, breast, and legs.

Reverse: All of the leaves will show detail but be worn on the ends.

ABOUT UNCIRCULATED

Obverse: Only a trace of wear will appear on Liberty's breast and knees.

Note: The clasp of Liberty's gown may be weak due to striking and therefore cannot be used to determine condition.

Reverse: Only a trace of wear will be visible on the ribbon bow and the tips of the leaves.

LIBERTY SEATED HALF DIMES
1860-1873

ABOUT GOOD

Obverse: The rim will be worn down into the letters and/or date.

Reverse: About half of the letters and/or design will be worn away.

GOOD

Obverse: There will be a full rim. "LIBERTY" will not show.

Reverse: There will be a full rim. The wreath will be worn flat.

VERY GOOD

Obverse: A total of any three letters (can be two full letters plus two half letters) of "LIBERTY" will be visible.

Reverse: Approximately half of the major detail will show in the wreath.

FINE

Obverse: There will be a full "LIBERTY" but it will not be sharp. Only the deepest folds of Liberty's gown will be visible.

Reverse: All of the major detail will be visible but will show definite wear.

VERY FINE

Obverse: "LIBERTY" will be sharp. More detail will be visible on the upper folds of Liberty's gown.

Reverse: Wear will be apparent on the top half of the bottom leaves.

EXTREMELY FINE

Obverse: There will be wear on Liberty's head, breast, and legs.

Reverse: There will be wear on the ends of the leaves and ribbon bow.

Note: There may be weakness due to striking at the top of the wreath. This weakness should not alter the grade of the coin.

ABOUT UNCIRCULATED

Obverse: Only a trace of wear will appear on Liberty's breast and knees.

Reverse: Only a trace of wear will be visible on the ribbon bow and the tips of the leaves.

DRAPED BUST DIMES
1796-1807

(For 1796-1797 reverses see page 48)

ABOUT GOOD

Obverse: The rim will be worn down into the stars, date, and/or "LIBERTY."

Reverse: The rim will be worn down well into the legend and design.

GOOD

Obverse: The rim may be worn down to the tops of the stars and legend. Head will be well outlined but worn flat.

Reverse: The rim will be worn down to the tops of some of the letters. The eagle will be clear but will show no detail.

VERY GOOD

Obverse: About 1/3 of the hair detail will show. Some drapery lines will be visible.

Note: On these early dimes some areas may show more wear than others due to uneven striking. This should not alter the grade of the coin.

Reverse: A few feathers will show in the eagle's wings. A partial "E PLURIBUS UNUM" will show.

FINE

Obverse: About half of the hair detail will show.

Reverse: About half of the features will show. "E PLURIBUS UNUM" may have a few weak letters.

VERY FINE

Obverse: About 3/4 of the hair detail will show.

Reverse: About 3/4 of the feathers will show and will be sharp.

EXTREMELY FINE

Obverse: Almost all of the hair detail will be visible, but portions may not be sharp due to striking.

Reverse: Wear will appear on the breast, tail, and at the ends of the wings.

ABOUT UNCIRCULATED

Obverse: Only a trace of wear will be visible on Liberty's shoulder and highest points of hair.

Reverse: Only a trace of wear will appear on the breast, tail, and at the tips of the wings.

Note: There may be weakness near the rims (especially on 1807 coins) due to striking. This should not affect the overall grade of the coin.

CAPPED DIMES 1809-1837

ABOUT GOOD

Obverse: The rim will be worn down well into the stars and/or date. The head will be worn smooth.

Reverse: The rim will be worn down well into the letters.

GOOD

Obverse: The rim may be worn down to the tops of the stars (usually only on one side). The head will be well outlined.

Reverse: All of the letters will be readable; a few of them may be weak.

VERY GOOD

Obverse: A total of any three letters (can be two full letters plus two half letters) of "LIBERTY" will be visible. The rim will be full.

Reverse: All of the letters will be sharp. A partial "E PLURIBUS UNUM" will show.

FINE

Obverse: A full "LIBERTY" will show. The ear will be visible.

Reverse: There will be a full "E PLURIBUS UNUM." About half of the eagle's feathers will show.

VERY FINE

Obverse: "LIBERTY" will be very sharp. About 2/3 of the hair will show.

Reverse: "E PLURIBUS UNUM" will be sharp. Almost all of the feathers will show, but wear will be visible on the high points.

EXTREMELY FINE

Obverse: All of the hair will show but will be worn on the highest points of the curls and around the face.

Reverse: Wear will be visible on the highest points of the feathers, claws, and neck.

ABOUT UNCIRCULATED

Obverse: Only a trace of wear will show on the shoulder and the hair above the ear and forehead.

Note: The clasp of Liberty's wrap may be weak due to striking and therefore cannot be used to determine grade.

Reverse: Only a trace of wear will be visible on the eagle's neck, left claw, and the tips of the wings.

DIMES 1837-1838 (no stars)

ABOUT GOOD

Obverse: The rim will be worn down into the field and may be worn into the date and/or head.

Reverse: About half of the lettering will be visible.

GOOD

Obverse: There will be a full outline of the Liberty seated figure. The shield will be worn smooth.

Reverse: The rim will be worn down to the tops of some of the letters.

VERY GOOD

Obverse: A total of any three letters (can be two full letters plus two half letters) of "LIBERTY" will be visible on the shield.

Reverse: There will be a full rim. The leaves in the wreath will be outlined but not well defined.

FINE

Obverse: There will be a full "LIBERTY" (including the letters "BE") on the shield, but it will not be sharp.

Reverse: The leaves will be separated but will show little detail.

VERY FINE

Obverse: "LIBERTY" will be sharp. Only the deepest folds of Liberty's gown will be visible.

Reverse: About half of the leaves will show detail.

EXTREMELY FINE

Obverse: There will be wear on Liberty's breast and legs.

Reverse: All of the leaves will show detail but will have wear on the ends.

ABOUT UNCIRCULATED

Obverse: Only a trace of wear will appear on Liberty's breast and knees.

Note: The horizontal lines of the shield are often weak, even on higher grades, due to striking.

Reverse: Only a trace of wear will be visible on the ribbon bow and the tips of the leaves.

LIBERTY SEATED DIMES
1838-1860

ABOUT GOOD

Obverse: The rim will be worn down into the date and/or stars.

Reverse: About half of the lettering will be visible.

GOOD

Obverse: There will be a full outline of Liberty. The shield will be worn smooth.

Reverse: All of the lettering will be full and sharp. The wreath will be worn flat.

Note: 1838-1860 Liberty seated dimes are usually seen with the reverse weaker than the obverse by at least one grade. This is due to the shallower die relief of the reverse.

VERY GOOD

Obverse: A total of any three letters (can be two full letters plus two half letters) of "LIBERTY" will be visible on the shield.

Reverse: The leaves in the wreath will be outlined but not well defined.

FINE

Obverse: There will be a full "LIBERTY" on the shield, but it will not be sharp.

Reverse: The leaves will be separated but will not show much detail.

VERY FINE

Obverse: The letters in the word "LIBER-TY" will be sharp. Only the deepest folds of the Liberty seated figure's gown will be visible.

Reverse: About half of the leaves will show detail.

EXTREMELY FINE

Obverse: There will be wear on Liberty's head, breast, and legs.

Reverse: All of the leaves will show detail but will have wear on the ends.

ABOUT UNCIRCULATED

Obverse: Only a trace of wear will appear on Liberty's breast and knees.

Note: The clasp of Liberty's gown may be weak due to striking (rather than wear) and cannot be used to determine condition.

Reverse: Only a trace of wear will be visible on the ribbon bow and the tips of the leaves.

LIBERTY SEATED DIMES
1860-1891

ABOUT GOOD

Obverse: The rim will be worn down into the letters and/or the date.

Reverse: The rim will be worn down into the wreath.

GOOD

Obverse: There will be a full rim. "LIBERTY" will not show.

Reverse: The wreath will be well outlined but will be worn flat.

VERY GOOD

Obverse: A total of any three letters (can be two full letters plus two half letters) of "LIBERTY" will be visible.

Reverse: Individual leaves will be outlined but show very little detail.

FINE

Obverse: There will be a full "LIBERTY" but it will not be sharp. The deepest folds of Liberty's gown will be visible.

Reverse: All of the major detail will be visible but will show definite wear.

VERY FINE

Obverse: "LIBERTY" will be sharp. More detail will be visible on the upper folds of Liberty's gown.

Reverse: Sharper detail will appear on the leaves of the wreath.

EXTREMELY FINE

Obverse: There will be wear on Liberty's head, breast, and legs.

Reverse: There will be wear only on the high points of the wreath.

ABOUT UNCIRCULATED

Obverse: Only a trace of wear will appear on Liberty's breast and knees.

Reverse: Only a trace of wear will be visible on the tips of the leaves.

Note: There may be weakness at the top of the wreath due to striking. This weakness should not alter the condition of the coin.

BARBER DIMES 1892-1916

ABOUT GOOD

Obverse: The rim will be worn down into the letters and/or date.

Reverse: The rim will be worn down into the wreath.

GOOD

Obverse: The letters will be complete. The head will be well outlined but will be worn smooth.

Reverse: The wreath will be outlined but worn flat.

VERY GOOD

Obverse: A total of any three letters (can be two full letters plus two half letters) of "LIBERTY" will show.

Reverse: Individual leaves will be outlined but will show very little detail.

FINE

Obverse: There will be a full "LIBERTY" on the head but it will not be sharp. The top of the wreath will be well outlined but the bottom will be worn.

Reverse: All of the major detail will be visible but will show major wear.

VERY FINE

Obverse: "LIBERTY" will be sharp. The wreath will be well outlined at both top and bottom.

Reverse: Sharper detail will appear on the leaves of the wreath.

EXTREMELY FINE

Obverse: The edges of the band on which the word "LIBERTY" appears will be distinct. The wreath will be bold. There will be wear above the forehead.

Reverse: There will be wear only on the high points of the wreath.

ABOUT UNCIRCULATED

Obverse: Only a trace of wear will appear on the hair above the forehead, the tips of the leaves in the wreath, and on the cheek bone.

Reverse: Only a trace of wear will be visible on the tips of the leaves.

VERY FINE

Obverse: Most of the major detail of the hair will be visible but worn on the high spots and around the face.

Reverse: 2/3 of the lines in the torch will show.

EXTREMELY FINE

Obverse: All of the hair detail will show but will have slight wear to the right of the forehead and above the ear. The ear will show complete detail.

Reverse: All of the lines in the torch will show. The flame will be well detailed.

ABOUT UNCIRCULATED

Obverse: Only a trace of wear will show on the cheekbone and on the hair above the ear.

Reverse: Only a trace of wear will show on the tops of the leaves and the high point of the flame.

TWENTY CENT PIECES
1875-1878

ABOUT GOOD

Obverse: The rim will be worn down into the stars.

Reverse: The rim will be worn well down into the letters.

GOOD

Obverse: There will be a full rim. The shield will be worn smooth.

Reverse: There will be a full rim. The eagle will be worn almost smooth.

VERY GOOD

Obverse: One or two letters of "LIBER-TY" will show.

Note: "LIBERTY" is raised on the 20c piece instead of incused as on the Liberty seated dime, quarter, or half dollar. Therefore, different grading standards must be used for the 20c coin.

Reverse: About half of the feathers will show on the eagle. The center of the breast will be worn smooth.

FINE

Obverse: Most of the word "LIBERTY" will show (with no more than 2½ letters missing), but will be very weak in spots. The major details of Liberty's gown will show.

Reverse: Almost all of the feathers will show. There will be a smooth spot in the center of the eagle's breast.

VERY FINE

Obverse: There will be a full "LIBER-TY." Liberty's gown will show considerable detail.

Reverse: All of the features will be visible but will show wear on the high spots.

EXTREMELY FINE

Obverse: "LIBERTY" will be very sharp. There will be wear on the breast and legs.

Reverse: There will be wear on the eagle's breast, left leg, and tops of the wings.

ABOUT UNCIRCULATED

Obverse: Only a trace of wear will appear on the head, breast, and knees.

Reverse: Only a trace of wear will appear on the eagle's breast and tops of the wings.

Note: The top of the eagle's right wing often (especially on 1875-CC) appears flat, even on Uncirculated coins, due to striking.

DRAPED BUST QUARTERS
1796-1807

(For 1796 reverse see page 93)

ABOUT GOOD

Obverse: The rim will be worn down well into the stars and "LIBERTY."

Reverse: The rim will be worn down well into the lettering and design.

GOOD

Obverse: The rim may be worn down to the tops of a few letters and/or stars. The head will be worn smooth.

Reverse: The rim will be worn down into the tops of some of the letters. The eagle's wings will be worn smooth.

VERY GOOD

Obverse: The head will be well outlined with the top and bottom curls distinct. No hair detail will show around the face or neck.

Reverse: A few feathers will show in the wings. A partial "E PLURIBUS UNUM" will show.

FINE

Obverse: About half of the major hair detail will show. There will be hair detail around the ear and to the left of the neck.

Reverse: About half of the eagle's feathers will show. About half of "E PLURIBUS UNUM" will show.

VERY FINE

Obverse: About 2/3 of the hair detail will show.

Reverse: 3/4 of the eagle's feathers will be visible. "E PLURIBUS UNUM" will be full.

EXTREMELY FINE

Obverse: All of the major hair detail will show.

Reverse: All of the major details of the feathers will show, but will be weak at the ends.

Note: The shield and eagle's wing or wings may be weak due to striking.

ABOUT UNCIRCULATED

Obverse: Only a trace of wear will show on the shoulder and the highest waves of hair to the left of the ear and forehead.

Note: The obverse of this series, particularly 1806 and 1807, is struck more softly than other denominations of this period.

Reverse: Only a trace of wear will appear on the eagle's breast feathers and at the tips of the wings.

LARGE CAPPED QUARTERS
1815-1828

ABOUT GOOD

Obverse: The rim will be worn down well into the stars.

Note: There may be partial "LIBERTY" lettering even in very low grades.

Reverse: The rim will be worn down well into the letters.

GOOD

Obverse: The rim will be worn down to the tops of the stars.

Reverse: The rim may be worn down to the tops of some letters. The eagle's feathers and the banner on which "E PLURIBUS UNUM" appears will be worn smooth.

VERY GOOD

Obverse: There will be a full rim. At least three full letters of "LIBERTY" must show.

Reverse: A partial "E PLURIBUS UNUM" will show.

FINE

Obverse: "LIBERTY" will be complete and sharp. Half of the major hair detail will show. All of the curls will be worn on the high points.

Reverse: There will be a full "E PLURIBUS UNUM" although a few letters may be weakly struck.

VERY FINE

Obverse: The hair will be more detailed. Drapery will be well outlined.

Reverse: "E PLURIBUS UNUM" will be sharp. About 2/3 of the eagle's feathers will show.

EXTREMELY FINE

Obverse: All of the hair will be detailed but will show wear on the high points.

Reverse: All of the feathers will be visible but the edges of the wings will show wear.

ABOUT UNCIRCULATED

Obverse: Only a trace of wear will show on the hair above the eye and ear and the tips of the curls.

Note: May be weakly struck around the curl on the neck and the drapery clasp; grade of the coin cannot be determined by these features.

Reverse: There will be a slight trace of wear on the tips of the wings and the claws.

SMALL CAPPED QUARTERS
1831-1838

ABOUT GOOD

Obverse: The rim will be worn down into the stars and/or date. The head will be worn smooth.

Reverse: The rim will be worn down into the letters. The eagle's feathers will be worn smooth.

GOOD

Obverse: The stars and date will be full. There may be a partial "LIBERTY."

Reverse: The rim may be worn down to the tops of a few letters. A few feathers will begin to show.

VERY GOOD

Obverse: There will be a full "LIBERTY" but a letter or two may be weak. Half of the major detail of the hair will show.

Reverse: The lettering will be bold. Half of the eagle's feathers will be visible.

FINE

Obverse: "LIBERTY" will be strong. All of the major hair detail will show but the curls will be worn flat.

Reverse: About 3/4 of the feathers will show but wear will be visible around the edges of the wings and on the neck.

VERY FINE

Obverse: The hair curls will show less wear and appear more rounded.

Reverse: All of the major details of the feathers will show. The leg, neck, and wings will show more detail.

EXTREMELY FINE

Obverse: Wear will appear on the highest hair curls and the top of Liberty's cap.

Reverse: Wear will be visible on the high points of the feathers and claws.

ABOUT UNCIRCULATED

Obverse: Only a trace of wear will show on the hair above the ear and around the forehead. The cheek will show slight wear.

Reverse: Only a trace of wear will show at the top and bottom tips of the wings and the eagle's left claw.

LIBERTY SEATED QUARTERS
1838-1891

ABOUT GOOD

Obverse: The rim will be worn down into the date and/or stars.

Reverse: The rim will be worn down well into the lettering.

GOOD

Obverse: There will be a full outline of the Liberty seated figure. The shield will be worn smooth.

Reverse: All lettering will be clear. The eagle will be worn smooth.

VERY GOOD

Obverse: A total of any three letters (can be two full letters plus two half letters) of "LIBERTY" will be visible on the shield.

Reverse: The rim will be sharply defined. A few feathers will show on the eagle.

FINE

Obverse: There will be a full "LIBERTY" on the shield but it will not be sharp.

Reverse: About half of the eagle's feathers will show.

VERY FINE

Obverse: "LIBERTY" will be sharp. Only the deepest folds of Liberty's gown will be visible.

Reverse: 3/4 of the feathers will be visible. Wear will show on the neck, leg, and edges of the wings.

EXTREMELY FINE

Obverse: More detail on Liberty's gown will show. There will be wear on Liberty's head, breast, and legs.

Reverse: All of the major details will be visible but will be worn on the high spots. The neck and claws will show slight wear.

ABOUT UNCIRCULATED

Obverse: Only a trace of wear will appear on Liberty's breast and knees.

Note: The clasp of Liberty's gown may be weak due to striking and cannot be used to determine condition.

Reverse: Only a trace of wear will show on the neck, the claws, and the tops of the wings.

Note: Flat spots will sometimes occur due to striking.

BARBER QUARTERS 1892-1916

ABOUT GOOD

Obverse: The rim will be worn down into the stars, letters, and/or date.

Reverse: The rim will be worn down into the lettering.

GOOD

Obverse: The stars, letters, and date will be complete. The head will be well outlined but worn smooth.

Reverse: The rim may be worn down to the tops of a few letters. The eagle will be well outlined but worn smooth.

VERY GOOD

Obverse: A total of any three letters (can be two full letters plus two half letters) of "LIBERTY" will show.

Reverse: A few feathers will show in the wings. A partial "E PLURIBUS UNUM" will show.

FINE

Obverse: There will be a full "LIBERTY" on the head but it will not be sharp. The top of the wreath will be well outlined but the bottom will be worn.

Reverse: About half of the feathers will show. "E PLURIBUS UNUM" will be 3/4 complete.

VERY FINE

Obverse: "LIBERTY" will be sharp. The wreath will be well outlined at both top and bottom.

Reverse: "E PLURIBUS UNUM" will be complete. More feather detail will show on the neck and tail.

EXTREMELY FINE

Obverse: The edges of the band on which "LIBERTY" appears will be distinct. The wreath will be bold. There will be wear above the forehead.

Reverse: All of the major detail of the feathers will show. Wear will be apparent on the neck, tail, and upper edges of the wings.

ABOUT UNCIRCULATED

Obverse: Only a trace of wear will appear on the hair above the forehead, the tips of the leaves in the wreath, and on the cheekbone.

Reverse: Only a trace of wear will be visible on the eagle's head, tail, and tips of the wings.

LIBERTY STANDING QUARTERS
1916-1917

ABOUT GOOD

Obverse: The date will be identifiable although it will be barely visible.

Reverse: The rim will be worn down into the lettering and stars.

GOOD

Obverse: The top portion of the date will be worn smooth. Date will be easily identified.

Reverse: All of the lettering will be clear. The eagle will be outlined sharply but will be worn almost smooth.

VERY GOOD

Obverse: The date will be complete but the very top will be weak. The band of cloth from Liberty's right hand to the shield will be outlined.

Reverse: 1/3 of the feathers will show.

FINE

Obverse: The date will be sharp. The shield will be complete around its outer edge. Liberty's right leg will be worn flat.

Reverse: Half of the feathers will show.

VERY FINE

Obverse: Liberty's right leg will be rounded but worn from above the gown to midway between the foot and knee. The gown line in the center of the upper leg will be worn.

Reverse: Almost all of the major detail of the feathers will show. The eagle's body and the front edge of the right wing will be worn flat.

EXTREMELY FINE

Obverse: Liberty's right leg will be worn on the knee. The gown line will be visible across the leg. The breast will be rounded.

Reverse: There will be wear on only the highest point of the front edge of the right wing. Wear will be visible on the highest points of the eagle's body.

ABOUT UNCIRCULATED

Obverse: Only a trace of wear will show on the knee cap, head, and center of shield.

Reverse: Only a trace of wear will be seen on the highest point of the eagle's body.

LIBERTY STANDING QUARTERS
1917-1924

ABOUT GOOD

Obverse: The date will be identifiable although it will be barely visible.

Reverse: The rim may be worn down to the tops of some letters.

Note: The lower grades are basically determined by the date, so the reverses appear to be in better condition than on quarters of 1925-1930.

GOOD

Obverse: Wear will extend into the date but the date will be easily identified.

Note: The date was on a higher plane from 1917 to 1924. Grading from About Good to Fine should be determined by the wear on the date.

Reverse: The rim will be worn down to the tops of the letters.

VERY GOOD

Obverse: The date will be complete but may be weak. The band of cloth from Liberty's right hand to the shield will be outlined on top.

Reverse: There will be a full rim. About 1/3 of the feathers will show.

FINE

Obverse: The date will be sharp. The shield will be complete around its outer edge. Liberty's right leg will be worn flat.

Reverse: Approximately half of the feathers will show.

VERY FINE

Obverse: Liberty's right leg will be rounded but worn from above the gown to the foot. About half of the mail covering the breast will show.

Reverse: The eagle's body will be worn smooth.

EXTREMELY FINE

Obverse: Liberty's right knee and the tip of her breast will show slight wear.

Reverse: All of the feathers will show but will be worn on the high spots.

ABOUT UNCIRCULATED

Obverse: Only a trace of wear will shown on the knee cap, breast, and center of shield.

Note: Usually struck with a flat head. An Uncirculated coin with a fully detailed head is worth a premium price.

Reverse: Only a trace of wear will show on the front edge of the eagle's wing and the high points of the breast.

LIBERTY STANDING QUARTERS
1925-1930

ABOUT GOOD

Obverse: The rim will be worn down into the date and letters.

Reverse: The rim will be worn down into the lettering and stars.

GOOD

Obverse: There will be a full date. The figure of Liberty will be worn smooth.

Reverse: The rim will be worn down to the tops of the letters.

VERY GOOD

Obverse: More detail will appear in the folds of Liberty's gown and on her shield.

Reverse: There will be a full rim. About 1/3 of the feathers will show.

FINE

Obverse: The shield will be complete around its outer edge. Liberty's right leg will be worn flat.

Reverse: Approximately half of the feathers will show.

VERY FINE

Obverse: About half of the mail covering the breast will show.

Reverse: The eagle's body will be worn smooth.

EXTREMELY FINE

Obverse: Liberty's right knee and the tip of her breast will show light wear.

Reverse: All of the feathers will show but will be worn on the high spots.

ABOUT UNCIRCULATED

Obverse: Only a trace of wear will show on Liberty's right knee and breast.
Note: Usually struck with a flat head.
Reverse: Only a trace of wear will show on the front edge of the eagle's wing and the high points of the breast.

WASHINGTON QUARTERS
1932 to date

ABOUT GOOD

Obverse: The rim will be worn halfway into the letters and date.
Reverse: The rim will be worn halfway down into the letters.

GOOD

Obverse: The rim will be worn into the tops of the letters and the bottom of the date.
Reverse: The rim will be worn down into the tops of the letters.

VERY GOOD

Obverse: The rim will touch the tops of the letters and the bottom of the date.
Reverse: The rim will touch the tops of some of the letters.

FINE

Obverse: There will be a full rim. The hairline will begin to show above the forehead.
Reverse: There will be a full rim. No feathers will show on the eagle's breast.

DRAPED BUST HALF DOLLARS
1796-1807

(For 1796-1797 reverses see page 93)

ABOUT GOOD

Obverse: The rim will be worn down into the letters, stars, and date.

Reverse: The rim will be worn down into the lettering and design.

GOOD

Obverse: The letters, stars, and date will be clear. The head will be outlined but worn smooth.

Reverse: The lettering will be clear although the rim may be worn down to the tops of a few letters. The wings will be worn smooth.

VERY GOOD

Obverse: About 1/3 of the hairlines will show.

Reverse: A partial "E PLURIBUS UNUM" will show. A few feathers will be visible.

FINE

Obverse: More detail will show in the hair; the hair will be 2/3 complete.

Reverse: Approximately half of the eagle's feathers will show. At least half of "E PLURIBUS UNUM" will show.

VERY FINE

Obverse: About 3/4 of the hairlines will be visible.

Reverse: "E PLURIBUS UNUM" will be full. About 3/4 of the feathers will show.

EXTREMELY FINE

Obverse: All of the major hair details will show. There will be flatness due to wear above the forehead and on the back of the head.

Reverse: All of the major details of the feathers will show. The ends and top edges of the wings will show wear.

ABOUT UNCIRCULATED

Obverse: Only a trace of wear will show on the highest points of hair, cheek, and shoulder.

Reverse: Only a trace of wear will show on the top edges and tips of the wings, breast, head, and tail.

CAPPED HALF DOLLARS
1807-1836

ABOUT GOOD

Obverse: The rim will be worn down into the stars and date.

Reverse: The rim will be worn down into the letters.

GOOD

Obverse: The head will be outlined but will show no detail. There will be a partial "Liberty."

Reverse: All of the letters will be complete. The eagle will be outlined but worn smooth.

VERY GOOD

Obverse: A full "LIBERTY" will show. About half of the major hair detail will be visible.

Reverse: A few feathers will be visible in the eagle's left wing.

FINE

Obverse: About 2/3 of the major hair detail will show.

Reverse: Half of the feathers will show. The eagle's claws will be well outlined but show wear.

VERY FINE

Obverse: All of the major hair detail will show. The tops of the waves of hair will be worn flat.

Reverse: Nearly all the major details of the feathers will show. Definite wear will show on the high points of the feathers.

EXTREMELY FINE

Obverse: The hair curls will be well rounded with wear only on the high points.

Note: The drapery clasp often is quite weak due to striking and should not be used to determine grade.

Reverse: All of the feathers will be clearly visible. There will be slight wear on the highest tips of the feathers, tops of the wings, and claws.

ABOUT UNCIRCULATED

Obverse: Only a trace of wear will appear on the cheek, cap, and highest waves of hair above the forehead and ear.

Reverse: Only a trace of wear will show on the claws, the tops of the wings, and the head.

Note: Weak striking may obliterate part of "E PLURIBUS UNUM" and the upper right wing. This weakness should not alter the grade.

REEDED EDGE HALF DOLLARS
1836-1839

ABOUT GOOD

Obverse: The rim will be worn down well into the stars and date.

Reverse: The rim will be worn down well into the letters.

GOOD

Obverse: The head will be outlined but worn almost completely smooth. There will be a partial "LIBERTY" showing.

Reverse: The eagle will be outlined but will show no feathers.

Note: The lettering on 1836 and 1837 halves will be weak due to a low rim. This must be taken into consideration when grading.

VERY GOOD

Obverse: There will be a full "LIBER-TY." A few waves of hair will show.

Reverse: A few feathers will be visible.

FINE

Obverse: About half of the major hair details will show.

Reverse: Approximately half of the feathers will show.

VERY FINE

Obverse: All of the major hair detail will show but the tops of the waves of hair will be worn flat.

Reverse: 3/4 of the feathers will show.

EXTREMELY FINE

Obverse: The hair curls will be well rounded with wear only on the high points.

Reverse: All of the feathers will be clearly visible but wear will shown on the high points. The claws and the edges of the wings will show wear.

ABOUT UNCIRCULATED

Obverse: Only a trace of wear will appear on the cheek, ear, cap, and hair above the forehead.

Reverse: Only a trace of wear will be visible on the highest edges of the wings, the head, and the claws.

LIBERTY SEATED HALF DOLLARS
1839-1891

ABOUT GOOD

Obverse: The rim will be worn down into the date and/or stars.

Reverse: The rim will be worn down well into the letters.

GOOD

Obverse: There will be a full outline of the figure of Liberty. The shield will be worn smooth.

Reverse: The letters will be complete although the rim may be worn down to the tops of a few letters. The eagle will be worn smooth.

VERY GOOD

Obverse: A total of any three letters (can be two full letters plus two half letters) of "LIBERTY" will be visible on the shield.

Reverse: The rim will be complete. A few feathers will show in the wings.

FINE

Obverse: There will be a full "LIBERTY" on the shield, but it will not be sharp.

Reverse: About half of the eagle's feathers will show.

VERY FINE

Obverse: "LIBERTY" will be sharp. Only the deepest folds of Liberty's gown will be visible.

Reverse: Nearly all the major details of the feathers will show. Definite wear will show on the high points of the feathers.

EXTREMELY FINE

Obverse: More detail of Liberty's gown will show. There will be wear on Liberty's head, breast, and legs.

Reverse: All of the feathers will be plainly visible. There will be slight wear on the highest tips of the feathers, the tops of the wings, and the claws.

ABOUT UNCIRCULATED

Obverse: Only a trace of wear will appear on Liberty's breast and knees.

Note: The clasp of Liberty's gown may be weak due to striking and therefore cannot be used to determine condition.

Reverse: Only a trace of wear will show on the head, claws, and tops of the wings.

BARBER HALF DOLLARS
1892-1915

ABOUT GOOD

Obverse: The rim will be worn down into the stars, letters, and/or date.

Reverse: The rim will be worn down into the lettering.

GOOD

Obverse: The stars, letters, and date will be complete. The head will be well outlined but worn smooth.

Reverse: The rim may be worn down to the tops of a few letters. The eagle will be well defined but worn smooth.

VERY GOOD

Obverse: A total of any three letters (can be two full letters plus two half letters) of "LIBERTY" will show.

Reverse: The rim will be complete. A few feathers and a partial "E PLURIBUS UNUM" will be visible.

FINE

Obverse: There will be a full "LIBERTY" on the head, but it will not be sharp. The top of the wreath will be well outlined but the bottom will be worn.

Reverse: About half of the feathers will show. "E PLURIBUS UNUM" will be complete although a few letters may be weak.

VERY FINE

Obverse: "LIBERTY" will be sharp. The wreath will be well outlined at both top and bottom.

Reverse: "E PLURIBUS UNUM" will be sharp. More feather detail will show on the neck and tail.

EXTREMELY FINE

Obverse: The edges of the band on which "LIBERTY" is located will be distinct. The wreath will be bold. There will be wear above the forehead.

Reverse: All the major detail of the feathers will show. Wear will be apparent on the neck, tail, and upper edges of the wings.

ABOUT UNCIRCULATED

Obverse: Only a trace of wear will appear on the hair above the forehead, on the tips of the leaves in the wreath, and on the cheek bone.

Reverse: Only a trace of wear will be visible on the head, tail, and tips of the wings.

LIBERTY WALKING HALF DOLLARS 1916-1947
ABOUT GOOD

Obverse: The rim will be worn down into the letters.   Reverse: The rim will be worn down into the letters.

GOOD

Obverse: The rim will be worn down to the tops of a few letters and the bottom of the date.
Reverse: The rim will be worn down to the tops of the letters.

VERY GOOD

Obverse: There will be a full rim. Half of the skirt lines will show (on 1921-1947 issues).
Note: From 1916 to 1920 the skirt lines are weak and cannot be used to determine grade.
Reverse: Full rim. A few feathers will show.

FINE

Obverse: More detail will show in the skirt lines (1921-1947) and in the leaves on the left arm.
Reverse: Half the feathers will show.

VERY FINE

Obverse: All skirt lines will show (1921-1947). The body will be well rounded and the breast
will be outlined.   Reverse: All wing feathers will show. Breast will be worn smooth.

EXTREMELY FINE

Obverse: There will be light wear on the head, breast, and left leg.
Reverse: High point of breast and left leg will be worn.

ABOUT UNCIRCULATED

Obverse: Only a trace of wear will show on the highest points of the head, breast, and left arm.
Reverse: A trace of wear will show on the breast, leg, and wing tip.

FRANKLIN HALF DOLLARS
1948-1963

GOOD

Obverse: The rim will be worn down into the lettering.
Reverse: The rim will be worn down into the lettering.

VERY GOOD

Obverse: There will be a full rim. Hair behind the ear will be worn smooth.
Reverse: The rim will be worn down to the tops of the letters.

FINE

Obverse: Some hair detail will show behind the ear. The cheek will be worn flat.
Reverse: There will be a full rim.

VERY FINE

Obverse: All of the major hairlines will show. The cheek will show wear but will be well rounded.

Reverse: About half of the horizontal lines on the bell will show.

EXTREMELY FINE

Obverse: More hair detail will show.

Reverse: 2/3 of the horizontal lines will show.

ABOUT UNCIRCULATED

Obverse: Only a trace of wear will be visible on the cheek, shoulder, and hair to the left of the ear.

Reverse: Only a trace of wear will show on the top of the bell and on the horizontal lines.

KENNEDY HALF DOLLARS
1964 to date

EXTREMELY FINE

Obverse: Wear will appear on the cheek and highest portion of hair to the right of the forehead.

Reverse: The head, shield, tail, and top edges of the wings will show.

ABOUT UNCIRCULATED

Obverse: Only a trace of wear will show on the cheek and highest portion of the hair.

Reverse: Just a trace of wear will appear on the neck and highest point of the tail.

FLOWING HAIR DOLLARS
1794-1795

ABOUT GOOD

Obverse: The rim will be worn down into the stars, legend, and/or date.

Reverse: The rim will be worn down into the lettering.

GOOD

Obverse: Liberty's head will be outlined but show no details. The stars, legend, and date will be clearly readable.

Reverse: The rim will be worn down to the tops of some of the lettering. The eagle will be worn smooth.

VERY GOOD

Obverse: Major facial details will be visible. The bottom strands of hair will show.

Reverse: The eagle's outline and the feathers around the body will be visible. The wings will be worn smooth.

FINE

Obverse: Approximately half of the major hair detail will show.

Reverse: The major feather details will show in the eagle's right wing.

VERY FINE

Obverse: 2/3 of the hair detail will show.

Reverse: Approximately half of the feather detail will show.

EXTREMELY FINE

Obverse: All of the major hair detail will be visible. The hair around the face and forehead will show wear.

Reverse: All of the major feather detail will be visible on the wings and tail. The breast will be smooth. The tips and edges of the wings will show wear.

ABOUT UNCIRCULATED

Obverse: Only a trace of wear will show on the tips of the highest curls and on the hair to the left of the forehead.

Reverse: Only a trace of wear will show on the head, breast, and tops of the wings.

Note: The breast feathers were usually weakly struck on this series. Many 1794 dollars are weakly struck at the lower left obverse and the corresponding part of the reverse. The hair detail is flatly struck on certain 1795 dollars.

DRAPED BUST DOLLARS   1795-1804

ABOUT GOOD

Obverse: The rim will be worn down into the stars, legend, and/or date.
Reverse: Rim will be worn down into the letters.

GOOD

Obverse: The head will be boldly outlined. There will be a full rim. Reverse: All letters will be readable.

VERY GOOD

Obverse: The bottom and top curls will show some detail. The rest of the hair will be worn smooth.
Reverse: Full rim. Partial "E PLURIBUS UNUM" (on large eagle).

FINE

Obverse: Approximately half of the hair detail will show.
Note: Drapery line details vary too much from one variety to another to be accurately used to determine grade. Reverse: Half of the feathers will show. "E PLURIBUS UNUM" will be weak.

VERY FINE

Obverse: 2/3 of the hair detail will show.   Reverse: 3/4 of the feathers will show.

EXTREMELY FINE

Obverse: All major hair detail will show. The highest waves of hair to the left of the neck and forehead will be worn.   Reverse: Slight wear on breast and top edges of wings.

ABOUT UNCIRCULATED

Obverse: Only a trace of wear will show on the bust, shoulder, and the hair left of the forehead.   Reverse: Traces of wear on breast and extreme top edges of wings.

LIBERTY SEATED DOLLARS
1840-1873

ABOUT GOOD

Obverse: The rim will be worn down into the date and/or stars.

Reverse: The rim will be worn down well into the letters.

GOOD

Obverse: There will be a full rim. The figure of Liberty will be sharply outlined. The shield will be worn smooth.

Reverse: The letters will be complete although the rim may be worn down to the tops of a few letters. The eagle will be worn smooth.

VERY GOOD

Obverse: A total of any three letters (can be two full letters plus two half letters) of "LIBERTY" will show on the shield. A few major gown lines will show.

Reverse: The rim will be complete. A few feathers will show on the wings.

FINE

Obverse: The "LI" and "TY" of "LIBER-TY" will be clearly visible but only the top of "BER" will show.

Note: The shield is raised higher on this series and thus shows wear more quickly than on the Liberty seated dime, quarter, or half. Different grading standards must be used.

Reverse: About half of the eagle's feathers will show.

VERY FINE

Obverse: "LIBERTY" will be complete with weakness showing only at the bottom part of "BE." All of the major gown lines will show.

Reverse: Nearly all of the major details of the feathers will show. Definite wear will show on the high points of the feathers.

EXTREMELY FINE

Obverse: "LIBERTY" will be sharp. The breast will be outlined but worn on the high points. The head and Liberty's right leg will show wear.

Reverse: All of the feathers will be plainly visible. There will be slight wear on the highest tips of the feathers, the tops of the wings, and the claws.

ABOUT UNCIRCULATED

Obverse: Only a trace of wear will show on the head, knee, and tips of the breasts.

Reverse: Only a trace of wear will show on the claws, head, and the tops of the wings.

MORGAN DOLLARS 1878-1921

GOOD

Obverse: The hair above the forehead and ear will be worn smooth.

Reverse: The rim will be worn down to the tops of the letters.

VERY GOOD

Obverse: The deepest strands of hair will be visible above the forehead. The hair above the ear will be worn smooth.

Reverse: Approximately 1/3 of the feathers will show on the eagle. The head and breast will be worn smooth.

FINE

Obverse: Approximately half of the hairlines will show from the top of the head to the ear.

Reverse: 3/4 of the major feather detail will show on the wings. The breast will be worn smooth.

VERY FINE

Obverse: 3/4 of the hairlines will show. The high points of the bottom curls will show considerable wear.

Reverse: All of the feathers will show on the wings. There will be wear on the center breast feathers and the top edges of the wings.

EXTREMELY FINE

Obverse: All of the hairlines will show. Wear will appear on the high points around the ear.

Reverse: There will be wear on the head and the highest points of the breast feathers.

ABOUT UNCIRCULATED

Obverse: Only a trace of wear will show on the hair just above the ear and the high points of hair above the forehead.

Reverse: Only a trace of wear will show on the highest points of the breast and head.

Note: Certain issues, particularly those of the branch mints, often come weakly struck on the eagle's breast, and allowance must be made for this in these instances.

PEACE DOLLARS 1921-1935

VERY GOOD

Obverse: The head will be worn smooth.

Note: This coin rarely is found in grades below Very Good.

Reverse: The word "PEACE" will show although a few letters may be weak.

FINE

Obverse: The high waves of hair above the forehead and ear will be worn flat.

Reverse: The right wing will be outlined but only a few feathers will show.

VERY FINE

Obverse: The hair above the forehead will be worn.

Note: The word "GOD" was often weakly struck. This does not affect the grade.

Reverse: The major details will show. Considerable wear will cause flatness on the right wing and head.

EXTREMELY FINE

Obverse: All of the hairlines will show. There will be some flatness on the highest waves of hair from wear.

Note: 1921 issues are in higher relief and often are found with weakly struck hair, even on top grade examples.

Reverse: All of the feathers will show, but not distinctly.

ABOUT UNCIRCULATED

Obverse: Only a trace of wear will show on Liberty's cheek and the highest waves of her hair above the forehead and ear.

Reverse: Only a trace of wear will show on the neck and the top outside edge of the right wing.

TRADE DOLLARS 1873-1885

GOOD

Obverse: The figure of Liberty will be well outlined but will be worn smooth.

Reverse: The motto "E PLURIBUS UNUM" above the eagle will be worn away.

VERY GOOD

Obverse: A partial "IN GOD WE TRUST" will show above the date. A few gown lines will show.

Reverse: A partial "E PLURIBUS UNUM" will show. About 1/3 of the feathers will be visible.

FINE

Obverse: "IN GOD WE TRUST" will be complete but will show weakness at the top. "LIBERTY" will also be complete although weak.

Reverse: "E PLURIBUS UNUM" will show although a few letters will be weak. Half of the feathers will be visible.

VERY FINE

Obverse: "IN GOD WE TRUST" and "LIBERTY" will be strong. The major details of the gown will be visible.

Reverse: There will be a strong "E PLURIBUS UNUM" but it will show definite wear. 3/4 of the feathers will be visible.

EXTREMELY FINE

Obverse: All of the gown lines will show, especially in Liberty's lap. There will be wear on the head, breast, and left leg.

Reverse: All of the feathers will be visible. Wear will show on the head, knee, and outer edges of the wings.

ABOUT UNCIRCULATED

Obverse: Only a trace of wear will appear on Liberty's left knee, tip of her left breast, and the hair above her ear.

Reverse: Only a trace of wear will show on the head, knee, and tops of the wings.

GOLD DOLLARS 1849-1854
TYPE I

FINE

Obverse: A full "LIBERTY" will be visible. The hair will be worn smooth all along the forehead and above the ear.

Reverse: The individual leaves will be well defined but fine details will not show.

VERY FINE

Obverse: The hair will be outlined above the forehead and around the neck.

Reverse: Some fine details will begin to show in the centers of the leaves.

EXTREMELY FINE

Obverse: All of the major hair detail will show. Wear will be visible only on the highest waves of hair.

Reverse: All of the leaves will show fine center detail. Wear will be visible on the tips of the leaves.

ABOUT UNCIRCULATED

Obverse: Only a trace of wear will appear on the tips of the curls above the forehead and ear.

Note: Gold coins (of all denominations) are rarely found in grades below Fine.

Reverse: Only traces of wear will show on the tips of the leaves.

GOLD DOLLARS 1854-1856
TYPE II

FINE

Obverse: The hair will be worn smooth above the forehead and ear. Some of the feathers will be worn almost smooth.

Reverse: The wreath will be boldly outlined but will show only major detail.

VERY FINE

Obverse: The hair will be outlined above the forehead and around the ear.

Reverse: Some of the fine leaf detail will begin to show.

EXTREMELY FINE

Obverse: All of the major hair detail will show.

Note: "LIBERTY" was often weakly struck on this series.

Reverse: There will be wear on all the high points of the wreath.

ABOUT UNCIRCULATED

Obverse: Just a trace of wear will show on the hair above the forehead.

Reverse: Only a trace of wear will appear on the tips of the leaves.

Note: The two center figures of the date often show severe weakness due to striking and should not affect the grade of the coin.

GOLD DOLLARS 1856-1889
TYPE III

FINE

Obverse: The hair above the forehead and ear will be worn smooth. The tops of the feathers will be smooth.

Reverse: The wreath will be boldly outlined but will show only major detail.

VERY FINE

Obverse: The tops of the feathers and the hair around the face will be well outlined.

Reverse: Some of the fine leaf detail will begin to show.

EXTREMELY FINE

Obverse: All of the major hair detail will show. Only a slight amount of wear will be visible on the tips of the feathers.

Reverse: Wear will be visible on only the high points of the wreath.

ABOUT UNCIRCULATED

Obverse: Traces of wear will show only on the tips of the feathers and on the hair above the ear and forehead.

Reverse: Just slight traces of wear will show on the tips of the leaves.

CAPPED QUARTER EAGLES
1796-1807

FINE

Obverse: Liberty's cap will be worn almost smooth. Only the deepest waves of hair will show.

Reverse: Only the deepest lines in the feathers will show. "E PLURIBUS UNUM" will not be sharp, although it will be readable.

VERY FINE

Obverse: The major detail of Liberty's cap will show. More hair detail will be visible.

Reverse: Most of the feathers will show but will be worn on the ends. "E PLURIBUS UNUM" will be sharp. The tail will show wear.

Note: "E PLURIBUS UNUM" may be weak in the center due to striking.

EXTREMELY FINE

Obverse: There will be wear on the tops of the curls by Liberty's neck and on the highest folds of her cap.

Note: There may be weakness due to striking in the center of the obverse.

Reverse: Wear will be visible on the head, tail, and upper edges and tips of the wings.

ABOUT UNCIRCULATED

Obverse: Only a trace of wear will be visible on the very top of the highest curls by Liberty's neck. A trace of wear will also be visible on the highest fold of her cap.

Reverse: Only a trace of wear will show on the tip of the head and the extreme upper edges of the wings.

BUST QUARTER EAGLES
1808-1839

FINE

Obverse: The hair above the forehead will be worn smooth. Only the deepest curls of the hair will show.

Reverse: About half of the eagle's feathers will show. The neck will be worn smooth.

VERY FINE

Obverse: "LIBERTY" will be very bold. All of the major hair detail will show.

Reverse: Considerable wear will show on the head, neck, and edges and tips of the wings.

EXTREMELY FINE

Obverse: Wear will be visible on the high points of the hair or cap above "LIBERTY" and on the curls around the neck.

Reverse: Wear will be visible on the head, neck, and upper edges of the wings.

Note: Weakness due to striking may appear on the eagle's right wing.

ABOUT UNCIRCULATED

Obverse: Only a trace of wear will show on the very highest tips of the hair and cap.

Note: The same hair rules for grading should be used for the three minor types in this series.

Reverse: Only a trace of wear will appear on the highest point of the upper edges of the wings and the highest feathers on the neck.

LIBERTY HEAD QUARTER
EAGLES 1840-1907

FINE

Obverse: "LIBERTY" will be complete but the "L" and "Y" may be weak. The hair curl on the neck, although outlined, will not show detail.

Reverse: About half of the feathers will show on the wings. The neck will be worn almost smooth.

VERY FINE

Obverse: "LIBERTY" will be bold. The major hair detail will show.

Reverse: 3/4 of the feathers will show.

EXTREMELY FINE

Obverse: Wear will appear on the tops of the waves of hair above the forehead and ear and on top of the head.

Reverse: All of the feathers will show, but there will be wear on the end of each feather.

ABOUT UNCIRCULATED

Obverse: There will be only a trace of wear on the hair above the ear and forehead.

Reverse: Only a trace of wear will be visible on the head just below the eagle's eye, the tips of the wings, and on the eagle's left claw.

INDIAN HEAD QUARTER EAGLES
1908-1929

VERY FINE

Obverse: The design on the band just above the forehead will be well worn and show only partial detail.

Reverse: The neck and upper end of the wing will be worn smooth. The feathers in the top half of the wing and breast will show wear.

EXTREMELY FINE

Obverse: The design on the band just above the forehead will be complete. Wear will be visible on the cheek, the feathers behind the ear, and the row of small feathers on top of the head.

Reverse: Wear will show on the neck, breast, and tip of the wing.

ABOUT UNCIRCULATED

Obverse: Only a trace of wear will show on the cheek. The small row of feathers will show wear on the tips.

Reverse: Only a trace of wear will be visible on the upper neck and on the tops of the feathers at the tip of the wing.

THREE DOLLAR GOLD
1854-1889

FINE

Obverse: The hair above the forehead will be worn into the bottom of the first few letters of "LIBERTY." The tops of the feathers will be worn smooth.

Reverse: The wreath will be boldly outlined but show only major detail.

VERY FINE

Obverse: The tops of the feathers will be well outlined but will show little detail. The hair above the forehead will touch "LI" of "LIBERTY."

Reverse: Some of the fine leaf detail will begin to show.

EXTREMELY FINE

Obverse: The hair above the forehead will be outlined but worn on the high point. All major details will show in the hair and on the feathers.

Reverse: There will be wear on all the high points of the wreath.

Note: The date may be weak due to striking.

ABOUT UNCIRCULATED

Obverse: A trace of wear will appear on the hair above the forehead and ear and on the tips of the feathers.

Note: The hair curls by the neck often come weakly struck and cannot be used to determine condition.

Reverse: Only a trace of wear will show on the ends of the leaves and the ribbon knot.

CAPPED HALF EAGLES
1795-1807

(For small eagle reverses see page 108)

VERY FINE

Obverse: The hair, cap, and bust will show wear on the high points.

Reverse: Most of the feathers will show although they will be worn on the ends. The tail will show wear.

EXTREMELY FINE

Obverse: Wear will be visible on the highest points of the cap, the hair above the forehead and to the left of the ear.

Reverse: Wear will be visible on the head, tail, and upper edges and tips of the wings. *Note: "E PLUBIBUS UNUM" may be weak in the center due to striking.*

ABOUT UNCIRCULATED

Obverse: Traces of wear will show only on the highest waves of hair above the forehead and behind the ear.

Note: The hair by the neck may be weakly struck.

Reverse: A trace of wear will show only on the extreme upper edges of the wings and the tip of the head.

BUST HALF EAGLES
1807-1838

VERY FINE

Obverse: "LIBERTY" will be very bold. All major details of the hair will show.

Reverse: Considerable wear will show on the head, neck, and ends of the wings.

EXTREMELY FINE

Obverse: Wear will be visible on the high points of the hair or cap above "LIBERTY" and on the lower hair curls.

Reverse: Wear will be visible on the head, neck, and upper edges of the wings.

ABOUT UNCIRCULATED

Obverse: A trace of wear will show only on the very highest tips of the hair and cap.

Note: The same basic rules for grading should be used for the three minor types in this series.

Reverse: Only a trace of wear will appear on the highest part of the upper edge of the wings and the highest feathers on the neck.

LIBERTY HEAD HALF EAGLES
1839-1908

FINE

Obverse: "LIBERTY" will be complete although the "L" may be weak. The hair will show considerable wear.

Reverse: About half of the feathers will show on the wings. The neck will be worn almost smooth.

VERY FINE

Obverse: "LIBERTY" will be bold. The major hair detail will show.

Reverse: 3/4 of the feathers will show. More detail will appear on the eagle's right leg.

EXTREMELY FINE

Obverse: Wear will appear on the tops of the waves of hair above the ear and forehead and on top of the head.

Reverse: All of the feathers will show but there will be wear on the end of each feather.

ABOUT UNCIRCULATED

Obverse: There will be only a trace of wear on the hair above the ear and forehead.

Reverse: Only a trace of wear will be visible on the head just below the eagle's eye, the tips of the wings, and on the eagle's left claw.

INDIAN HEAD HALF EAGLES
1908-1929

VERY FINE

Obverse: The design on the band above the forehead will be well worn and will show only partial detail.

Reverse: The neck and upper end of the wing will be worn smooth.

EXTREMELY FINE

Obverse: The design on the band just above the forehead will be complete. Wear will be visible on the cheek, the feathers behind the ear, and the row of small feathers on top of the head.

Reverse: Wear will show on the neck, breast, and tip of the wing.

ABOUT UNCIRCULATED

Obverse: Only a trace of wear will show on the cheek. The small row of feathers will show wear on their tips.

Reverse: Only a trace of wear will be visible on the upper neck and on the tops of the feathers at the tip of the wing.

CAPPED EAGLES 1795-1804

VERY FINE

Obverse: The hair, cap, and bust will show wear on the high points.
Reverse: Most feathers will be visible but will be worn on the ends.

EXTREMELY FINE

Obverse: Wear will be visible on the highest points of the cap and on the hair above the forehead and to the left of the ear. Reverse: Wear on head, breast, and upper edges and tips of wings.

ABOUT UNCIRCULATED

Obverse: Only traces of wear will show on the highest waves of hair above the forehead and behind the ear. Reverse: Traces of wear on extreme edges of wings, tip of head, and breast.

LIBERTY HEAD EAGLES
1838-1907

FINE

Obverse: "LIBERTY" will be complete but the "L" may be weak. The hair will show considerable wear.

Reverse: About half of the feathers will show on the wings. The neck will be worn almost smooth.

VERY FINE

Obverse: "LIBERTY" will be bold. The major hair detail will show.

Reverse: About 3/4 of the feathers will show.

EXTREMELY FINE

Obverse: Wear will appear on the top of the waves of hair above the forehead and ear and on top of the head.

Reverse: All of the feathers will show but there will be wear on the end of each feather.

ABOUT UNCIRCULATED

Obverse: There will be only a trace of wear on the hair above the ear and forehead.

Reverse: Only a trace of wear will be visible on the head just below the eagle's eye and on the tips and extreme upper edges of the wings.

INDIAN HEAD EAGLES
1907-1933

VERY FINE

Obverse: Considerable wear will show on the feathers just above the word "LIBER-TY" and on the hair above the ear and forehead.

Reverse: 3/4 of the eagle's feathers will show. Wear will be visible on the head, top of the left wing, and high points of the legs.

EXTREMELY FINE

Obverse: Slight wear will show on the hair and on the feathers just above the word "LIBERTY."

Reverse: Less wear will show on the left wing, head, and legs.

ABOUT UNCIRCULATED

Obverse: There will be a trace of wear on the highest waves of hair above the ear and eye.

Reverse: Only a trace of wear will be visible on the tip of the left wing and tip of the head.

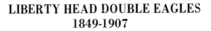

LIBERTY HEAD DOUBLE EAGLES
1849-1907

FINE

Obverse: The hair on top of the head and below the coronet will be worn smooth. The curls by the neck will show only major details.

Reverse: The eagle's head will be worn smooth. The tail and the tops of the wings will show considerable wear.

VERY FINE

Obverse: The major hair detail will show on top of the head and below the coronet.

Reverse: All of the feathers will show on the wings but they will not be sharply detailed.

EXTREMELY FINE

Obverse: Wear will show on the curls by the neck and on the hair above the ear and below the coronet.

Note: The hair curl directly under the ear will sometimes be weak due to striking. Carson City issues usually lack the detail of coins from other mints.

Reverse: The feathers on the wings will be sharp. Wear will be visible on the head, neck, tail, and the highest points of the shield.